To Eva
8-21-04
a gift to you

Dot Hoelscher

COMMENTS ABOUT LION CROSSING THE SINAI:

"I strongly recommend to the Lions of the world ... that they should read and learn from your experiences. They will enjoy reading and at the same time benefit from your philosophy of life. It will certainly give them an extensive insight into Lionism."—**Kajit Habanananda, Bangkok, Past International President**

"Ebb Grindstaff is an old friend and a new author. He has done himself proud on both accounts."—**Ann W. Richards, 45th Governor of Texas**

"[Lion Crossing the Sinai] appears to be very interesting, especially as we have been in the same job and met the same people. Get it printed!"—**Sten Akestam, Stockholm, Past International President**

"... This is an autobiography and also a 'Here I Stand' declaration of personal values ... A striking part of the story is the large number of civic and charitable undertakings of the Lions ... I am glad to recommend the book to all who know Ebb Grindstaff, or who are interested in Lions International, or who just wish to meet a real West Texan."—**Angus S. McSwain, Professor of Law, Baylor University (Retired)**

"Lessons learned from this Lion leader are many. He is a true example of servant leadership always making difficult choices for his life purpose, balancing family, business and service. It is amazing what a difference one person from Ballinger, Texas, can make. Encourages anyone to strive for their dreams."—**Kay Baker, President, Kay Baker Presentations**

"A rich and fascinating journey, weaving international events, Lionism, and public speaking into delightful reading."—**Don Reynolds, 21st Century Forecasting**

"Ebb Grindstaff, a Past President of Lions Clubs International, takes the reader on an odyssey that details a remarkable life of dedication and commitment to his family, to the legal profession and to volunteerism to his community, his state, his nation and the world. His life story is told with unabashed honesty and in a candid manner that reveals an extraordinary Texan accomplishing extraordinary things to benefit humanity. It's a great read!"—**Judge Brian Stevenson, Past International President**

Lion Crossing the Sinai

A West Texan's Global Experiences in Leadership and Service

Everett J. "Ebb" Grindstaff

1982-1983 President of Lions Clubs International

With Sam Pendergrast

SUNBELT EAKIN ★ SE Austin, Texas

For CIP
information,
please access:
www.loc.gov

FIRST EDITION
Copyright © 2002
By Everett J. "Ebb" Grindstaff
Published in the U.S.A.
By Sunbelt Eakin Press
A Division of Sunbelt Media, Inc.
P.O. Drawer 90159
Austin, Texas 78709-0159
email: sales@eakinpress.com
website: www.eakinpress.com
ALL RIGHTS RESERVED.
1 2 3 4 5 6 7 8 9
1-57168-681-9

This book is dedicated to:

My loving parents Judge and Atha Marie Grindstaff, as without their guidance, patience, and example, any of these successes would not have been possible. They provided the principles for living, home, church, education, and service;

my wife Jeannette ("Jay") who has been a steadying force for me in all of our endeavors—but especially during all of our travels as she was, in my opinion, the most gracious and charming first lady of Lionism. None of my success would have been possible without her. She has survived both the mountaintop of experiences and has gone through the deep ravines and valleys with dignity and grace;

and the grassroot Lion who gives unselfishly to his fellow man and is the true hero in the trenches of volunteer service to his fellow man and those less fortunate than he.

Contents

Acknowledgments

There is no way to thank all the people who have assisted me, not only in the compiling of this book, but also in my half-century Lionism career, my legal career, my family, and my alma mater, Baylor University.

I know I'll omit some people—and I hope they will accept my humble apologies and my enormous gratitude for their contributions, influence, and assistance. You know who you are, and I simply convey to you my heartfelt gratitude. None of us are supreme or indispensable, and it is only by working together that we're able to serve those who might be less fortunate.

Isaiah 40. 31: "They that wait upon the lord shall renew their strength. They shall mount up with wings like eagles. They shall run and not be weary. They shall walk and not be faint."

To J.C. Gore, long-time law enforcement officer and now chief of police in the city of Ballinger, thanks for the reproduction of pictures contained in this book.

Thanks again, Judge, Herb Petry, and Tex Mayer for your advice, direction, and encouragement.

Thanks to Roy Schaetzel, executive director of Lions Clubs International; Elsa Vaintzettel, secretary-treasurer of the International Association; Will Wilson, past executive director when I was an international director; and to the most dedicated group of individuals or Lions that I have ever known.

Any success that we had during those years would not have been possible without the guidance and dedication of the area and regional representatives: 1–Vispy Engineer, India and Southeast Asia; 2–Johnny Kim, Korea, now deceased; 3–Jim McLardie, Australia, New Zealand, and Indonesia; 4–Juan Weiss of Peru, South America; Shing-Fa, Tsai, Taiwan; and 5–David Saunders, England and Ireland; 6–Kleber Obin, France; 7–Loredona Mandelli, Italy.

All the past presidents of our association, both those deceased and those still alive, are active in our international organization (they all stand tall and still take an active part in all the conventions, and can be called upon for able advice at any time), and each one of them is unique in their personalities and philosophy of service. Each one performs such service as will best serve their fellow man. To each of them, from myself and the organization, many thanks for your contributions.

I also must say a special thanks to Past International President Murakami, deceased, and at that time 2nd Vice President Joe Wrobleski from Pennsylvania and 3rd Vice President Bert Mason from Ireland, for their support as officers while I was going through the chairs and also their contributions to Lions Clubs International when they were presidents. They were absolutely a tower of strength in the support of our programs.

Another one of my mentors and idols during the time I was a young Lion and on into the years as I approached the presidency was Robert Roy Keaton from Weatherford, Texas (near where my dad was born). Roy Keaton—whose articles in the Lions magazine I cut out while I was in high school and college and some of whose ideas I used for my programs and in my inaugural speech—was a great inspiration and fantastic speaker. Roy was a dynamic leader in the formative years of Lions Clubs International. During his membership the Lions grew from 380,000 to more than 600,000 members and Lions Clubs spread from 28 to 102 countries.

Chapter 1

Long Way from Ballinger

As a nearly lifelong resident of Ballinger, Texas, I've taken occasional ribbing from friends who happen to know I was born in nearby Abilene.

Of course, I don't remember the actual occasion, but I guess I correctly learned a few important things. Nevertheless, it is always good to return to Ballinger, no matter how well you've been received elsewhere.

Most people are likely to treat you well wherever you are, but everybody tends to have their own agenda that may or may not coincide with yours.

You never know whom you're going to meet or what will be expected of you; And it's always good to carry a few changes of underwear and some chocolate when you get far from home. After that first trip to Ballinger, I seemed destined to be a traveler—particularly since I had lawyer uncles in Rotan and Weatherford and grandparents in Abilene. And my Dad (always called "Judge" after he was first elected in Runnels County in 1940 and then served fifteen years as district attorney for Runnels and Tom Green County), spent lots of time on the road.

But nobody in Ballinger, Abilene, or San Angelo could have predicted in 1931 that this kid from West Texas would find him-

1

self in Cairo, Egypt, forty years later, trying to get to Tel Aviv, Israel—much less that he would be meeting two Middle East leaders and recognizing their attempts at peace in the perpetually combative area.

Having been selected by the executive committee of Lions International to present awards of honor to Anwar Sadat of Egypt and Menachem Begin of Israel, I felt it was my responsibility to present the awards as quickly as possible.

After that, the mission became complicated.

The original plan had been to meet with Sadat on a Saturday, but had to be postponed because of some tactical conflict in the regional unrest. Still I expected to meet with Sadat on Sunday morning and fly from Cairo to Tel Aviv that afternoon and make the award to Begin shortly after.

The telephone system in the Land of the Pharaohs was no help as it might take two or three hours to complete a communication. But I soon found out not only was there no daily flight between Cairo and Tel Aviv—there was no alternate route through Turkey, Cyprus, or Italy.

One plus factor was my wife Jeanette (better known as "Jay"), who had been with me during the two-week, seven-nation tour for the executive committee and was ready to cross the Sinai with me to make the presentations. I can't say either of us was fully hopeful about the trip, and I can't recall—in our twenty-six years of marriage before that and another seventeen since— seeing Jay less talkative. But she was ready, and so was I.

The easy part—if there was one—was getting to Sadat's villa about an hour and a half from Cairo.

I spent half an hour with President Sadat, who was cordial and relaxed and made me feel the same. After a while it seemed like I was talking to the guy next door. But I couldn't help being thrilled as I gave him the large plaque known as the "Head of State Award," the highest governmental honor of Lions International. The presentation was half of the unusual joint award to Sadat and Prime Minister Begin and reflected the Lions respect for their courage in seeking peace among long-hostile neighbors.

In fact, the world news of that very weekend was that Iraq had attacked Iran, and it was not known how the Egyptian

President Sadat and the Israeli Prime Minister Begin would react to each other—much less to a visitor from Ballinger, Texas.

Fortunately, I had put in a lot of miles between West Texas and Baylor University in Waco as a youth, during a hitch in the Far East with army intelligence for postgraduate work, and many thousands more miles with the Lions Club before I found myself in the dust and the uncertain roads littered with abandoned artillery in the Sinai with a commitment to talk peace with two people who knew more about war and hostilities than peace or Texas.

I had logged countless miles and scores of countries for meetings of the Lions and was the third vice president of Lions International with 1.3 million members, so I had learned something about travel and leaders.

Now I'd need all I knew and then some . . .

My meeting in Jerusalem on a Tuesday morning seemed impossible. My patience, not noted for its duration, was beginning to wane, but my alter ego, Jay, had always maintained that "there has to be a way to do anything you need to do," and we kept trying.

I couldn't get in touch with my contact person in Jerusalem; I called the Lions executive administrator in Chicago, Roy Schaetzel, who could talk to Israel directly. It happened to be midnight in Illinois at the time, but Roy is another can-do type of Lion, and he undertook the challenge to coordinate new travel plans with the district governor in Israel. By that time, it seemed the only possibility was for us to cross the Sinai Peninsula by car. (When Schaetzel told the Israelite Lion I was going to cross the Sinai by car, the district governor said, "What? No one has ever done that . . ."

But, on the strength of Jay's encouragement, we were going to do it.

The plans were that we would leave Egypt at 2 P.M. on a Sunday. However, since the Egypt–Isreal border closed at 5 P.M., we arranged for a car and driver for 2 A.M. Monday for what should be the six-hour trip to Tel Aviv. The moonlight crossing would put us in the Sinai desert at the most comfortable time and still let us arrive at the Israeli capital on Monday morning.

But, at best, Sinai time is not like Ballinger time, and for starters the driver showed up twenty minutes late, accompanied by a companion who was seriously ill or on drugs or both. His head shook constantly, making Jay and me both uneasy.

We arrived at the Suez Canal at 5:40 A.M.—still allowing twenty minutes to catch the ferry.

Sinai drivers are not like Ballinger drivers. This driver decided to have breakfast before the crossing. Meanwhile, the mysterious traveling companion got out of the car and approached a ferry official and entered into heated conversation—in Arabic—the gist of which turned out to be that foreigners were not allowed to cross the canal by car at this point.

By the time the driver returned, he, his argumentative companion, Jay, and I were taken to the police station.

After some twenty minutes more of sometimes heated discussion, I remembered I was carrying a newspaper with an article about our award to President Sadat.

Nobody was much impressed, and soon we were all escorted to another office that seemed like our FBI, but an FBI-type official escorted us down to the canal and accompanied us onto the ferry. We were back in motion, two hours late.

Jay was not having a picnic, and my outer composure was not entirely authentic as we sped through ranks of guns and bigger guns and all-too-many grim-faced men who seemed ready to shoot at something. Trying to make up for lost time, our driver cruised at about ninety miles an hour along roads reminiscent of Runnels County forty years earlier.

Our cool early morning trip had turned into a 100-degree, high-noon bake that wasn't improved when the windows were opened. What passed for a gritty breeze reminded us we were in one of the world's great deserts on a four-hour tour through camels, mud-and-stick huts, and more abandoned artillery.

What had seemed a simple change of cars at the Israeli border wasn't a lot more fun.

Where was the car that was supposed to meet us? The driver didn't know. What if the car didn't show? The driver didn't know.

But there was supposed to be a bus we could catch on the other side.

Jay and I hadn't yet learned to pack for a three-week trip

and had too many suitcases—which I had to carry on several gauntlets through customs.

And the bus stop was a rock beside the road where the bus might stop.

But Jay's faith was in operation, and a bus came. We loaded our luggage among chickens, goats, and nearly wall-to-wall people.

When we got to the other side, unloaded it all, and were heading through customs again, we were surprised by a wonderful English phrase: "Are you the Grinstaffs?"

It was the people who had been waiting for us for hours. They said they could have met us on the other side if they'd only known.

We arrived at Tel Aviv that afternoon—more than twelve hours after we left Cairo on a six-hour trip.

Prime Minister Begin was not as relaxed as Sadat had been—understandably, since he received me on his way to an emergency meeting to deal with the Iraq attack on Iran.

But he seemed to appreciate the Lions honor, and he agreed when I told him Sadat had been hopeful about the prospects for peace in the area.

He gave me an autographed copy of his autobiography *Revolt,* and I breathed a sigh of relief at being able to complete my Lions Club mission in a troubled corner of the globe at a troubled time.

Jay and I took rest and recreation with a trip to the Holy Lands before coming home to Ballinger. Nazareth and the rest of that storied land was not only any Christian tourist's dream trip but also an impetus to long-term cogitations about questions of war and peace, leadership and service, and the meaning of life on this ancient, varied, and ever-changing world.

It wasn't until we traveled up the Jordan River and saw additional signs of hostilities and wars that we better understood things. When we arrived at the southern shore of the Sea of Galilee we had tea with the mayor and the president of the local Lions Club—who was to escort us to Nazareth. During tea, he handed us a map and said it might assist in our travels. It turned out to be a map of Texas. The president of the Nazareth Lions Club was a highway engineer who had been to Austin, Texas, twice for conferences and seminars and noted in the biographical information that I was a graduate of Baylor Law School. This small gift was a gesture of peace and understanding in a troubled world.

At the time it seemed pretty plain: Begin and Sadat were unquestioned leaders not only (or least of all) politically but because they had a vision for better times in an area that had known some of the worst and people who had endured the ravages of deserts and demons near and far.

None of us could have known for sure that both the leaders I met and admired that busy weekend would give their lives literally and bloodily for that quest, but both of them surely recognized the mortal threat—and they forged ahead with their mission. Sometimes survival is not the greatest good—as both Sadat and Begin demonstrated later by giving their lives toward their peace efforts in that troubled sector of the world.

My contribution to the triangle of relationships on that Sinai weekend was certainly more in the line of service. But—despite my awareness that I was a Colorado River lad presuming to cross the Suez—I was not without examples and experiences and lessons in service. My actions were built upon experience from the Boy Scout troop of Ballinger through the campus efforts with leadership at Baylor and U. S. Army training and sometimes covert assignments in Counterintelligence in the Far East to years of brotherhood and training, and leadership and service in the ranks of Lions International.

And it is the distillation of half a century in such experiences and insights that I hope to share in this book.

Because most of us, particularly in the global society which is developing whether we like it or not, are likely to find ourselves crossing the Sinai in one way or another. (And the horrifying experiences of September 11 changed our world from a safe and secure America to another world with much of the same threats and fears of those places over there. More than ever we are all in this together and forced to think more of our one world.)

Have a good trip—and hopefully a good read.

Chapter 2

All Right, I Started in Abilene

I was a fairly latecomer to Ballinger, and I've been razzed about it by some Ballinger "natives."

I was born in Abilene, Texas, on May 7, 1931, and Ballinger turned out to be my third hometown. My second residence was in Maverick, where we moved in September of 1931 when Mom and Dad took school jobs there.

They both went to Hardin-Simmons; the Baptist college—at that time a half century in operation—was Abilene's major school. I think Mom graduated in 1927 and Dad a year later

Both families were in the food business.

My dad, Judge, moonlighted at Mr. Poole's café near the post office and then at his own place over on South First Street—one of the busier streets in town because it was also old Highway 80, known for many decades as the "Broadway of America," which accounts for the hundreds of downtown businesses from Texarkana to El Paso named Broadway this or that.

Mr. Poole's menu featured hamburgers, but he was most famous for his chili—the recipe which Dad passed on to me with the promise that I would give it to nobody but my children. It is my oldest kept promise. And the all-time record for business had

7

to be when the young guy named Lindberg landed his first in-tercontinental airplane, the "Spirit of St. Louis" out east of town.

In 1915, Mother—born Atha Marie Porter to James A. and Cora Porter—had come with her parents to Abilene from Fort Worth at about seven years of age to start Porter's Dairy and truck farm where Pine Street runs into the Anson Highway.

One of my first legal cases was in 1957, when part of the dairy was condemned for highway construction. Much earlier, I received my first commercial experience peddling Grandpa Porter's cantaloupes and watermelons along Pine, Hickory, and brick-paved Grape streets during summer visits to Abilene. There were little family stores in most neighborhoods in those days, to which we delivered produce. However, many customers picked up their milk and vegetables at the dairy. The Porters had about ten or twelve stalls for milk cows, and there were other small dairies around town.

Grandma Porter helped around the dairy and was a house-wife who made great biscuits.

It was good experience in business for me. All the money from the sales was kept in tin cans or jars. It was my first lesson in integrity as it certainly was tempting for a ten- to twelve-year-old lad to borrow a little money from the cookie jar. However, I would not dare, as I had this strange feeling my grandparents knew within a few pennies as to the content.

To me it was a grand old farm with melons, cantaloupes, chickens, cows, pigeons, and even a friend or two my age down the road.

My mom Atha Marie graduated from Abilene High School.

The elder Grindstaffs moved to Abilene about 1930. He had a café on the west side of Oak Street about two blocks south of Thornton's, the landmark department store that covered the nearby block south of the Taylor County courthouse (now the site of the city-county police building). The café was in business during World War II, when Camp Barkeley's location west of town started turning Abilene into a city. I remember Grand-mother Grindstaff's great pies well into the 1950s—and the fact that she always took me to the sparkling new Paramount theater on Christmas afternoon.

My dad developed "Everett's Chili" at Poole's Café, while

he was at Hardin-Simmons. (I still make it a couple of times a year, but not as hot as Dad's, which would melt your gooze . . .)

A cousin who did the family tree tells me the Grindstaffs came to America in 1738 from Germany. They landed at Philadelphia and migrated down the Shenandoah Valley to what was then North Carolina. My branch probably came from eastern Tennessee and my great-grandparents were Elijah and Hannah Emeline Oberholser Grindstaff—married September 24, 1871, in Carter County, Tennesee. My great-great-grandparents were Michael M. Grindstaff, who lived in Hempton, Tennessee, all his life, and his wife Sarah who gave birth to nine children while living in a two-room frame house on thirty acres of land.

When we moved to Maverick, Mom had already taught school one year at Coahoma and one year at Lawn, and Dad taught, coached, and swept out the building at Union Grove School before they got married June 10, 1930, in Abilene.

I was three months old when Dad was hired as superintendent of the four-teacher Maverick school for $150 a month. Mom was one of the teachers, at $125 a month. I recently ran across a class photo that included ten students, probably the senior class.

Mother's aunt, Ora Jones, moved with us to Maverick and kept me while Mom and Dad were at school.

We lived next to the school in the teacherage at Maverick, which helped a lot during the Depression, when the school sometimes ran out of cash and had to pay in warrants that would be accepted by grocers and other merchants. Maverick was its all-time biggest then, I guess, with a barber shop and auto mechanic store in addition to the food store. I remember going to San Angelo a time or two for a movie—which seemed like a major treat and a long trip at the time.

But Dad wanted to practice law, so while we were at Maverick he started studying for the bar exam. Judge always said he was not going to look at the back end of a mule all his life. There were no lawyers in Maverick, but he would go to Austin in the summers for studies at the University of Texas Law School and borrow books for study after school duties. He passed the bar in 1934.

That same year, neighbors talked him into running for county school superintendent, and it was the beginning of a life-long affair with politics.

There were thirty-three independent school districts in Runnels County at the time, and it was a major political post, but Dad won a tough race over two other men in the non-partisan campaign by going all over the county, visiting every farm—often helping with the plowing, changing tires, or other chores.

His salary rose to a couple of thousand dollars a year, and we moved to Ballinger, the county seat, where he served in that post for six years. He had to run every two years, but he was never opposed again.

It was 1940 before Dad got back to the law for which he had studied so hard. He ran for county judge in another tough race, but when he won he also earned the title of Judge, and Everett Clinton Grindstaff became known simply as Judge Grindstaff until he died in 1992 at age eighty-eight.

Ballinger was also where I met one of my best friends, Walter Hill, the son of county attorney Roy Hill.

Walter and I made all the ice cream socials, cake walks, and get-togethers where the old folks were campaigning, and we learned how to cadge extra ice cream and treats by catching a crowd of citizens talking to one of our dads and asking for treats while they were busy politicking. Walter played football for Texas A&M and graduated from that university, spent a couple of years in the service, and then retired from General Dynamics (now Lockheed) in Fort Worth, but we still share great memories of working the political gatherings at nine years old.

The county superintendent's office was good training for grassroots politics; Dad learned to meet people and understand the issues. The issues were not all that different: roads, books, buildings, salaries, and buses. But the problem with books was not so much the content as how to pay for them, and school buses were a fiscal matter instead of racial.

Each of the thirty-three school districts had a board of trustees—and they took their independence seriously, but Superintendent Grindstaff was the focal point for building, staffing, and curriculum problems. And there was an annual late summer migration to his office for books, which were paid for in part by the state but stored in Ballinger and zealously sought by thirty-three schools.

Mom taught for thirty-three years—she always said she taught for thirty-three years and never got out of the third grade—most of them in Ballinger. During the early years she taught in what was called the Mexican school in south Ballinger, where she shared pedagogical duties with Eva Tucker, a Hispanic whose husband was in the oil business. Eva, at this writing, is still living in San Angelo and has been a philanthropist for several causes in San Angelo. Recently a tribute to the Hispanic population in Ballinger was held at the West Texas Collection at Angelo State University. It was certainly good to visit with Eva who is in her late eighties but still active in several different charitable causes. The Mexican school was a good school, and you can bet my mother was as loving and dedicated a teacher as any across town.

The Mexican school was integrated toward the end of World War II, but I've always been indebted to my early associations through my mother that saved me from the prejudice that has troubled many people and communities.

Dad served as county judge from 1940 until 1951, and he was never opposed after the first race.

In 1951 he was appointed district attorney for Runnels and Tom Green counties, where he served another fourteen years. He worked mostly in San Angelo, but we continued to live in Ballinger, and Earl Smith, the other district attorney, lived in San Angelo.

Judge Grindstaff hired Aubrey Stokes fresh out of Baylor Law School as an assistant, and Aubrey later replaced Smith as the Angelo DA.

The DA could also practice privately in those days, and Judge Grindstaff and I formed a partnership in 1956. Judge retired from the DA post in 1965, and we continued to share the practice until his death in 1992.

But Judge was always interested in politics—an interest I inherited from such highlights as a 1940 visit in Austin and on the courthouse lawn at Ballinger (at one time known to be the largest in the state of Texas) with Governor W. Lee O'Daniel to talk about bonding to remodel the courthouse in Ballinger.

"Pappy Lee," the colorful populist with the flour company and the unsinkable band, the "Light Crust Dough Boys," was hard to top, but we enjoyed working and visiting with the likes of Governor Buford Jester and Railroad Commissioner Olin Culberson—in the latter of whose home we always ate on Thanksgiving when we'd go to the University of Texas ball games.

I'd always expected to go to UT to study law and room with Bob Agnew (another good friend growing up and his mom Treva was like a second mom), but after I graduated from Ballinger High School in 1948, I visited Baylor and was impressed with its friendliness and size. The school was about the same size as the city of Ballinger then. I moved to the Waco school for six years—three for undergraduate and three for law school.

The spring of 1954 was a busy time for me.

I took my finals at Baylor one week in March, passed the bar exam the next week, married Jeannette White of Fort Worth (my "Jay") on April 3, and was drafted into the army on June 10th.

In preparation for the bar examination, one of my friends and law buddies, Brad Corrigan of Hamilton (who later practiced law in Dallas) decided we needed to start studying several months prior to the test. We did not need any interruption, so we traveled to Hamilton, where we had the luxury of Mrs. Corrigan's home cooking; then we'd drive down to the beautiful Leon River, where we studied and asked questions from previous bar examinations and tests from Baylor. We also studied the advance sheets of appeals to the Supreme Court because many reports indicated there would be questions from the advance sheets.

Then we went to Austin and the state capitol building and into the legislative chambers and the space behind the presiding officer's stage—for those of us who needed to type their exams.

They handed out the bar exams, and I nearly passed out as the typewriters started to pound around me and I had not read one-third of the first question. We finished, and even though we would not receive the result for two or three months, we both passed the first time. In fact, we were so excited we began tearing the paper-bound advance sheets—not one question from which had been on the tests—and throwing them out on the highway. We were littering—for the first and last time in my life—but we felt we deserved it.

Two months later, on June 10, I was drafted into the U.S. Army and after basic training was sent to Fort Holabird, Maryland, Counterintelligence Corps, and then on to Japan for the Korean Police Action.

I took basic training at Fort Bliss in El Paso in June of 1954—and I didn't know it at the time, but the weather in that great but high-desert area had to be some of my most effectual preparation for crossing the Sinai years later.

I remember Jay came to visit me in El Paso and later admitted she was shocked to see me with a burr haircut, lips swollen from the exposure, and covered with sand.

We went to a motel, where I was going to clean up and change clothes for a little sightseeing, but I made the mistake of lying on the bed for a moment. Jay let me sleep for hours before I got back to life and a quick trip to El Paso and Juarez.

Chapter 3

Born to Be a Lion

Only my family and my hometown are older and dearer to me than Lionism.

As with most good things in my life—my dad showed the way. He joined the Ballinger Lions Club in 1935 when the club was about six years old, and he was district governor in 1946—when there were only five Texas districts, instead of the present sixteen, and over 700 in the world. I was in high school in 1946 and was deeply impressed when Dad took me along to Philadelphia that year for the Lions International Convention— and the next year to San Francisco. When I, as a son, became district governor in 1964, Judge and I were the first father-and-son district governors in Lions Club International according to the research done by several people.

It was in San Francisco that I met another of the most influential men in my life, Herb Petry of Carrizo Springs, Texas, who was elected third vice-president of Lions International at that world session. Three years later, in 1951, he traditionally became international president—in his case the youngest in history.

Herb not only served as a sterling example of leadership and service but actively took me under his wing. He was not only a peerless Lion but a great politician and public servant. After UT Law School with the likes of John Connally and Lloyd Bentsen, he served as chairman of the Texas Highway Commission for several years, the longest in history. (Sadly, Petry died the same year as my Dad and Tex Mayer, in 1992.)

I took a break from Baylor in 1952 to attend the International Convention at Mexico City, where I met and danced with another distinguished and prettier Texan. She was Kathryn Grandstaff, who was a campus beauty at UT and later married Bing Crosby. Her father was both a Lion and a county commissioner in West Columbia.

I started my Lions career that same busy month of March 1954, by joining the Ballinger Lions Club.

The Lions met at noon at the historic old Central Hotel until it was razed, and I enjoyed attending meetings with Dad, who was then district attorney as well as past Lions district governor.

Another great meeting for Dad and me was with the late Melvin Jones, who was credited with founding Lions International in Chicago. The first International Convention was in October of 1917, at the Adolphus Hotel in Dallas. There was confusion about who did what first and where, but there was never any doubt that Melvin Jones started it all.

Dad and I met Jones in Houston, probably at a district governors meeting, and one of the great honors of any Lions career was to be named a Melvin Jones Fellow sometime later. In 1984, when I was chariman of the Melvin Jones foundation, we had a first Melvin Jones Foundation luncheon when forty to fifty attended—now several hundred attend.

But I had another kind of service to take care of first.

I had been drafted into the U. S. Army in 1954, and I was on the road again. I was assigned to the Counterintelligence Corps in Japan after basic training and CIC training at Ft. Holabird, Maryland, near Baltimore. I had applied for the judge advocate general staff, but I received word of my acceptance— and an officer's commission—after I was established with the CIC and told I would have to serve a longer enlistment for the JAG. As I did not intend to make the army a career, I said, "No thanks," and settled for the CIC—and five days later received orders for Japan, which seemed like the end of the world at the time.

I took my whole first $99 paycheck and rented an apartment, where Jay joined me after six weeks. She got a job with the army telephone service and had to take a bus, a subway, and a cab (on rainy days) to get to work downtown; but she had been a trouper from the start, going with me to Baltimore where I was in training at Ft. Holabird and working in the sportswear department at Hutzler's—a big department store where her purchases exceeded her salary, but her appearance made it all worthwhile.

I was assigned to the Rightist Section of the CIC where we investigated individuals or groups who desired to return the emperor to power, versus the Leftist Section who investigated Communists.

My work was surprisingly dull in some respects for such a cloak-and-dagger title, but I was asked to teach English to the officers at the downtown police station and that helped pass the time. Again, my experience and insight had been broadened by travel and association with many different people, customs, and attitudes.

During vacations—and nearly every weekend—we traveled around Tokyo and Yokusa and took one long trip on the bullet train to Kyoto, Naro, and Osaka; we saw hundreds of shrines and many, many pagodas and learned a lot about the cultures of Japan.

We lived in a little apartment in the suburbs—known as Ku's—of North Tokyo that was close to the CIC compound. The commissary where we shopped because of the prices was on the far west side of Tokyo. Jay and I would meet there to buy groceries, and the subway trips were wild—particularly after Jay was pregnant. The Japanese are very polite if they know you, but it's everyone for himself on the subway, and we seldom got home with the groceries intact after I'd had to push Jay onto a car and try to set myself and the groceries in the door before the train moved. I've played a little football, but it was never as rough as the Tokyo subway. It was a great experience for us—an international experience, a global experience—and it was probably a big help in our International Lionism politics and policy.

Ironically, the only Japanese Lion president in my experience was Kay Murakami, who served before and after me until he passed away right after his presidency while he served as the immediate past president.

We were very glad to say "sayonara" to the Far East in 1956 and get back to Ballinger, where I could take up practice in the new law firm of Grindstaff and Grindstaff.

I resumed active participation in the Lions Club and joined the Ballinger Jaycees—where I was president in the late 1950s when we received the State Project of the Year Award for an old-time political rally and birthday celebration at the airport with a parade and dinner on the grounds and lots of politicians from Congressman Henry B. Gonzales on down.

I was named Balliger Lions Club president in 1960, and four years later, district governor of District 2A-l, and I visited all sixty-four clubs from Kingsland to Midland to Ballinger and to Ozona. This seemed like a lot of territory, but it didn't compare with Dad's district in 1946 that had ranged from Ballinger to Brownsville.

My first International Convention as district governor was at Toronto in 1964. One of the most important and satisfying projects of my life developed in 1969, when I was named president of the Lions Crippled Children's Camp at Kerrville, which was operated and financed totally by Texas Lions and free to all the children.

The camp was chartered in 1949 and opened in 1953 with free camping for blind, deaf, and orthopedically handicapped children. There were many polio victims in those days, and the camp was what convinced me of the value and the magic of the world's largest service organization.

As of the summer of 2001, there had been some 38,000 children served at the camp, including some 10,000 diabetics since 1971—according to the office of Executive Director Stephen Mabry.

You can't visit the camp—much less get hands-on involvement—without being a better Lion and a better person. It is rewarding to see the smiles on the faces of children on crutches or in wheelchairs—or with an arm missing or some other handicap—as they join in the activities of baseball or arts and crafts, or even are lowered by winch into the pool for a swim. It is also rewarding to see—as we first saw in the early seventies—a diabetic child giving himself a shot that he had never done at home, because at the camp Johnny was sitting next to him and giving himself a shot.

The smiles you see on these kids, the thank-you's, and the dedication of the counselors all fulfill one of the inscriptions on the front gate from the Bible. The inscription, in effect, conveys the message that in as much as you have done it unto the least of these, you have done it unto me.

Prior to traveling to Colorado to work on the final draft of this book, I went up to the semi-annual meeting of the district governors and the meeting of the Crippled Children's Camp at Kerrville, Texas. It's usually during the last camping session for either the handicapped or the diabetic camp; this particular year it was the diabetic camp. As I was entering the administration building, I heard some joyful noises over at the outdoor amphitheater. The camp was full that weekend because the diabetic children were being picked up by their parents and all of the Lions were there.

I asked somebody what was going on and was told it was the awards ceremony for the diabetic children. Something drew me to that particular area where I had been involved in the initiation of the diabetic program in 1970-1971 and on through Lions Clubs International. I knew I would be late for my meeting, but I went over to the area where a long walk sloped up to the top and then sloped down to the seats and the stage.

I went to the top and observed the joyful laughter and antics of the children and started back to the administration building when my eye caught sight of a young lady coming up the ramp. She had one hand on the railing and a crutch at a forty-five-degree angle and was ambulating with difficulty up the ramp.

I decided I would talk to her, but as I approached she talked to me first. "Hi there, how are you doing?" I was taken aback. I said I was doing fine and looked back up the ramp and thought about the distance she had to go. I knew from other experiences with kids and individuals that they would not accept any help. I said, "Well, it's a long way up there on a hot day."

She raised her head and looked without hesitation and said, "Yes, it is, and it's also hot, *but I'm going to make it*."

I said, "Yes, I know you will." I noticed the name on her nametag was Kelly, and when I talked to the executive director I found out she was a counselor and a great inspiration to all the kids and other counselors, just as she had been to me.

The Lions Camp was started basically as a summer operation, but in the sixties we became involved with the Texas Blind Commission and started the massive training program for the blind in the winter months. It became up close and personal for me during a visit there with Frank Robertson, the executive director, one of the most outstanding individuals I ever knew and who happened to be blind. As we were talking, he said, "There's Hash . . ." (a blind young man from Ballinger). I hollered, "Hash, how're you doing?" He said, "Just great . . . I've got my bat and ball and I'm fixing to go out and play baseball and I'm sure going to have a good time." This is yet another example of great benefits given free to children because of Lions who are willing to give of themselves, their time, and their efforts to make good things happen.

Frank Robertson was also a past district governor and was responsible for the early development of the camp; Stephen Mabry is the present president executive director and has done an outstanding job during this program. Other executive directors have been Past District Governor Jimmy McPherson from Houston and Glen Crawford, who was the executive director prior to Stephen Mabry.

One of my greatest inspirations during the furtherance of the diabetes program had to be one of my most favorite people, Ruth Farebee Clark. I first met her at a Lions Club Forum and had the most interesting conversations prior to her presentation—at which time she did not know that I was incoming president of the Lions Clubs International. However, we had a mutual subject that bound us together; however, hers was of actual experience. Later, I would again have the opportunity to hear Ruth at the closing sessions of a forum. She had some kind remarks to make and dedicated a song to me and presented me a rose. I subsequently had the opportunity to meet with her and her husband to share some of her latest developments. In addition to being an outstanding speaker, she is a caring and loving person and has one of the most outstanding attitudes that one could have.

Yes, Ruth has diabetes and has had one or two transplants, along with a heart problem, that I recall, during one of these operations, yet she had competed very successfully in the World Transplant Games in America and Australia and other places, and she and her husband survived a devastating accident in 1990. Still, she was a winner in every way and has far outlived all predictions of her previous transplants and other medical problems. She has lived through them with a smile on her face, and you would never think her boring. I guess God had a purpose for Ruth—not only in my life, but to the entire diabetic program.

It appears that I have always been influenced by someone with diabetes even though I have never had diabetes. However, it was only in the midst of writing this book that I read an article in the Austin Downtown Lions magazine about Ruth Shugart presenting a program on diabetes. I immediately congratulated her by letter concerning her program, and she sent me a book, *Challenge to Win* by Nancy Shugart, which was a most interesting and outstanding book about the many challenges and opportunities Ruth faced in the years from her youth up to finally being able to read on the CCTV machine furnished by the Lions Club. The book also included details of the inspiration she received from the Hadley School of the Blind in Chicago.

It now seems odd, but the diabetes camp took some salesmanship in 1970 and 1971, because diabetes was a condition that people didn't talk about much. Even families with affected members tended to keep it quiet, dealing privately with their doctors and specialists and doing a lot of home treatment and controls.

I traveled around the state for a year, selling the program to Lions and helping educate our own members and the public about the serious health problem that didn't get much public attention.

We received excellent cooperation from Dr. Luther Travis of the University of Texas at Galveston, which was operating a pioneer juvenile diabetic program at Friendswood, Texas. This program eventually merged with the diabetes camp at Kerrville.

And as of this writing, Dr. Stephen Ponder was donating his services, time, and advice not only to the operation of the camp; as well he prepared a video on diabetes and diabetic care that is being produced for distribution to the school systems funded by the Texas Lions Foundation.

And the work goes on. As of this writing, an expansion program expected to cost from $2.5 to 5 million will make Kerrville a truly premiere camp—financed through contributions from the Lions Club International Foundation and Lions Clubs, districts, and individuals all over the state.

And there are other Lions camps. While I was an international director in 1972-1974, we visited Licola in Australia, whose founders had visited Kerrville to study our program as a pattern for theirs—as have many camps in America and throughout the world.

The Kerrville camp was my inspiration to introduce diabetes as an international Lions project. My work with the Lions camp in those years stimulated fellow Lions to encourage me to be a candidate for international director in 1972. I had never thought about running until PDG Charlie Phillips from Humble suggested the race, and other influential Lions encouraged it.

In leadership, as elsewhere, timing really can be everything, and that kind of timing had been going on in other areas for me—such as the State Bar of Texas, when one of the fifteen state directorships was open and I was elected in 1971 and served through 1974.

In fact I got the State Bar of Texas to meet in a cotton patch in Runnels County. In one of our meetings in Austin, I suggested that we have a West Texas legal seminar at Phil Lorfing's Steak House in Lowake, but they couldn't find it on a map and said nobody would show up. Dallas and Houston and Austin had always been the sites. But I persisted—noting there was an airstrip in a cotton patch across the road from Lowake—home of long-famous West Texas steaks and refreshments—and I guaranteed a large crowd because lawyers from San Angelo, Abilene, Midland, Odessa, Abilene, and Brownwood would come to a "Cotton Patch Conference." They would come because of a steak meal and some of the presenters could take advantage of the landing strip in a cotton patch across the road. Two hundred and twenty-five lawyers showed up—compared with fifty or sixty in Dallas and Houston for such events. And I haven't been to another legal seminar yet with 225 people.

During that time I had served as Ballinger city attorney since 1957—a post I still held as of this writing—in addition to practicing law and being involved with Lions and camp activities between meetings.

I was really a busy Ballingerite after 1972, when I was asked to run for a post as Lions International Director.

The International Convention was in Mexico City that year, and we came up with the slogan "Ride the Ebb Tide"—illustrated with thousands of little boxes of Tide detergent passed out to everybody at the convention. Roy Minear and Carl Hyde were the campaign chairmen for the election for international director in Mexico City. There could not have been any two better people—along with Evelyn Minear and Lou Hyde. They devoted two years to formulating and planning literature, brochures, stickers, give-aways—in addition to crossing the state, as there was a tough campaign going on within the state for international director; Pat Whitaker of Hillsboro was a formidable candidate until he withdrew in February prior to the election in May.

We cleaned up at Mexico City, and I came home with another wide-ranging job for two years.

Probably as a result of my pursuit internationally of such issues as diabetes and my service on the Board, I was approached about running for third vice-president—the traditional track to the international presidency.

Past International President Herb Petry, past International Director Tex Mayer, and Past International Director Don Buckalew were among my backers—as was lawyer John Petry of Carrizo Springs. They and others helped me test the waters for a 1977 candidacy for the third vice-president post. But the timing didn't seem right, so we came back to Texas and again went around the state getting endorsements from all the districts.

I was elected third vice-president at Montreal in 1979 and was on the ladder toward the presidency.

My dad gave the seconding speech—a gesture that was warmly appreciated by the family-oriented Lions—and particularly by his proud son.

It was during my term as third vice-president that I found myself in Egypt in 1979 trying to cross the Sinai peninsula to carry the message of peace and hope to two troubled but determined leaders.

I was installed as international president at the Atlanta convention 1982, and it was pretty inspiring to make a speech to some 20,000 people. It was probably one of the better speeches I ever made because I worked on it a long time—and it helped that it was the first time we used a teleprompter on the podium.

With the advice and help of experts like Herb Petry and Tex Mayer, my preparation extended beyond the speeches to a good foundation for the two major special projects of my administration—international projects in diabetes control and anti-drug efforts.

Texas Lions got involved against drugs in the late seventies, with the wisdom and experience of General Robbie Risner (chairman of the Texas drug program, a friend of Ross Perot, and a participant in the International Convention at Hawaii) along with Past District Governor Lin Rose and Lion John Hall, who were innovators and pushers of the drug program for the Texas Lions, as were so many dedicated Lions.

A major thrust of the diabetes program was our "Journey for Sight," which was a meaningful banner because diabetes is the number one cause of blindness. I shall always be grateful to Norm Dahl from Illinois who was serving as an appointee to the Board. We were able to promote boat races, ski races, scooter races, sled races, bicycle races, runs, walks, jogs, and the like as fund-raising projects for the "Journey."

Much of the funding has gone to research and education, and I have taken pride in the fact that my two special projects have far outlasted my administration and the Lions are involved in both programs in some form.

The anti-drug program has been heavily educational as well as preventive. Particularly effective has been the project known as "Quest," in which at-risk youths are provided with life skills and learning skills to better equip them to avoid getting into drugs in the first place.

Dr. Carlton Turner was most helpful in the anti-drug program with his experiences and efforts against the world scourge of drugs during the administration of President Ronald Reagan. I met Mr. Reagan, along with Mrs. Reagan, during their "Just Say No" drive that was an important adjunct to our Lions anti-drug program.

Lions, ideally, serve for today but also build for the future, and I was gratified to be instrumental, along with the officers and board and countless Lions, in two such key programs that are still important to Lions.

I remember when we became involved with the worldwide diabetes program. It was said that Japan didn't have a problem with diabetes. But years later, I found myself sitting behind a Japanese Lion who turned out to be a diabetic. His name was Kay Murakami, who was immediate past president while I was president of Lions International. Kay and his wife Shoko were great friends and Kaoru Anderson, his interpreter, was fantastic in their support. Kay and Kaoru and I spent many late hours visiting on policy and procedures. My tour in Japan was beneficial to understanding their culture.

When stones are launched into the water, you never know how far the ripples will go.

Chapter 4

Great Role Models

I have never understood people who cannot stand being involved in a lot of projects, and I know why. Mother and Judge were involved in community activities as long as I can remember, and other people I respected encouraged the same involvement.

The Judge's job as superintendent at Maverick was full time enough, with full charge of a five-teacher school; and Mother was one of the teachers. Of course, it was the depth of the Depression and nobody had any money to spare, but with the Judge's $150 monthly check and Mothers's check for $125, we lived comfortably—particularly since we lived rent-free in the teacherage that belonged to the school.

It was there I began to learn the value of a dollar, but I now realize we were a lot easier entertained in those days. I only remember a couple of trips to San Angelo for a movie. Even fifty cents for a movie and maybe a sack of popcorn was not a minor expense—not to mention the seventy-mile drive to and from San Angelo. Mostly, we stayed home and entertained ourselves with books—often from the school library—and Texas History, which later made it easier for me to do well in school.

But Judge and Mother made it clear from the start that the

way to get ahead in life was to study hard and work hard and be ready for whatever opportunities might emerge.

It was a little like osmosis for me to acquire the realization that no matter what your talent, if you studied hard and worked hard you could compete with anybody. And, on reflection, I guess I didn't have a lot of natural talent for books and school-work, but it never occurred to me not to work as hard as I could at whatever I was doing. It paid off with good grades in school and elsewhere.

Half a century later, it's still some of the best advice received—along with what they're now calling family values, such as honesty and integrity and self-discipline and helping one another.

Persistence and determination were the Judge's specialty. He used to say he learned them from staring over a plow at the back of a mule or the hungry mouth of a cotton sack. It was that kind of view that helped him decide to become a lawyer—that and the fact that two of his uncles around Parker County were teachers and later lawyers. In fact, both Uncle Lige and Uncle Henry were seniors in the law class of 1913 at the University of Texas.

He didn't mind burning the midnight oil many nights in Maverick, Texas, during school years. That may have been literally, because I remember a lot of kerosene lamps somewhere in my childhood, though I guess we had electricity in the teacher-age at Maverick because it was on the school grounds.

I remember the Judge studying nights, out of law books he borrowed wherever he could—many of them from the University of Texas Law School, where he would spend his summers in law classes. I recollect he studied in Austin summers from 1931 to 1934.

His after-school law study taught me the value and the fascination of reading. I still remember some of those school books on Texas history—like the picture books of Stephen F. Austin and Sam Houston, two pretty hardworking and determined guys who gave us the state of Texas. The Judge's library included self-help works by authors like Dale Carnegie and Napoleon Hill.

The Judge's influence went far beyond printed pages, and I guess I was most impressed with his involvement in all phases of life—from the schools, where he was everything, to the First

Baptist Church, where he was a Sunday school teacher for years and Sunday school superintendent. He was also active in the Lions Club. He was certainly involved in all phases of community life, being responsible for the remodeling of the courthouse in 1940 and obtaining Bruce Field—a primary military training base for Ballinger—also in the early forties.

As a teacher for thirty-three years, Mother always said she taught for thirty-three years and never got out of the third grade—which was true. But at home she also instilled in me certain qualities—such as the importance of yard work. She even arranged for me to get yard work for neighbors that I understood I was to complete in an efficient and excellent matter—and indicated that was to be the same goal for any job.

Because both my parents were working, I had my share of household chores—which I didn't really enjoy, but I knew that was what I was supposed to do. During the war, Mother also helped me plant a "victory garden" with extra vegetables to sell to neighbors.

The same attitudes applied to school work. I was not Einstein, but I didn't think of bringing home bad grades, because that would not be the right school ethic. Even though I had to study harder than some, I brought home good grades—and it was all my own work.

Mother instilled in me values and virtues in all phases of life and all relationships with my fellow students. She always emphasized that I should never go with a girl that I would not marry. I was pretty fortunate in that respect, and I got the best one for life.

Mother was always involved in a teachers association and Ballinger's Carnegie Library—currently still in operation and one of the last of the original century-old monuments to a steel man who believed in getting involved.

Mother also helped organize the 36th Study Club which later became the Ballinger Womens's Club.

So it's little wonder I was inclined to be involved in volunteerism.

But the Judge always had time to encourage me—in fact, he made it clear he wanted me to go further than he did—and that's why he was so proud of what happened to me in Lionism.

He could never have known how impressed I had been with his work—even in Lionism, because it had been quite a feat for him to be district governor back in the forties. In fact, I still think he was just about the perfect example of what a Lion—and a man—ought to be. I never heard him say anything bad about anyone—and not just because he was in politics; he just didn't believe negativity accomplished anything.

He never met a stranger. Everybody knew and loved the Judge.

It was not that things came easy to him either. Speaking was one of his great fears, but he did it whenever he had to, and he did it well. He told me that sometimes he was scared to death about making some speech or other, but he had to do it. In fact, he thought you had to be a little scared to make a good speech.

He encouraged me to take declamation at Ballinger High, and I won the district championship. Sometimes I forget to mention I was the only entrant that year, but I did have to make a speech, and I learned from it.

I'll never forget the 1948 regional meet in old Abilene High—the great old building on South First at Grape in Abilene that has been Lincoln Junior High for years.

When I walked out on that stage, glanced up, and saw I was standing right under that big old eagle, I forgot it was the symbol of the Abilene Eagles, but I knew exactly how the Judge felt about speaking. My knees were knocking so much I was reminded of a friend of mine who had a wooden leg that went to knocking when he rose to speak.

I don't even remember how I scored, but simply getting there was something else.

Above all, the Judge taught me the work ethic, because I started working every summer as far back as I can remember.

It was one thing I tried to pass on to my son, Jeff, and he has had both a strong work ethic and base values.

My first big job as a kid was carrying water to the carpenters who were building some barracks for Bruce Field, the primary training base at Ballinger that was our major contribution to the war effort. I was about ten at the time.

Later—and hotter and harder—I had a job that was called "oiling mesquite," which consisted of pouring kerosene on the brush and trees to kill the pesky water-sappers (which I recall sometimes when I see chefs paying more for mesquite wood than the cows were worth when I was killing mesquite). I did that for a couple of summers, then I started working for the Triple AAA program, a precursor of the Federal ASC-type program. I measured peanuts and cotton and did some work with people building tanks and terraces.

I worked for the State Highway Department for three summers. I did anything that was hot: shoveling pre-mix, running some equipment, and waving the flag to keep motorists from running over the state workers. I've been over some of those roads time and time again, between Bronte and Robert Lee and some in downtown Ballinger, and I remember that hard work and think about how well some of those old roads have served thousands of drivers for half a century.

Meanwhile, we had a family farm—raising mostly sheep— that I worked, too. I spent most of the time going back and forth for parts and thinking about why I didn't want to be a farmer.

Finally, my last summer at Baylor Law, 1953, I went to school to get on track to graduate in March 1954.

Baylor offered another rare example in leadership and service—Judge/President Abner McCall, a great man who was involved and taught others to be involved, had some first-rate credentials. Judge McCall, whose middle name was practically "Service" for a full life as a law professor, also served in Texas government, education, and law enforcement.

Like many of his generation, McCall had come up the hard way—the really hard way—starting as an orphan with his brother in the Masonic Home in Fort Worth, where he graduated as class valedictorian. (Gene Keel and his wife, Nell, were products of the Masonic Home; they lived in Ballinger where Gene was a pharmacist for over forty years.)

At the age of eighteen, McCall showed up at Baylor in 1933 with just a few dollars in his pocket but a yen to be a lawyer.

Graduating at the head of his law class in 1938, he scored higher on the Texas Bar Exam than any other applicant before him. In 1948 he became head of the law school from which he had graduated only ten years earlier.

In 1956, then Texas Governor Allan Shivers named McCall

to a seven-month interim appointment on the Texas Supreme Court. He labored for more power for the court to disbar unethical lawyers and also cracked a menacing whip at the unethical practices of questionable trust and insurance companies.

He served as dean of the law school until 1959.

He was vice-president of Baylor from 1959 until 1961 and president from 1961 until 1981—when he was named chancellor and later president emeritus in 1985.

Will Davis, my Baylor roommate in law school, said at Judge McCall's memorial service: "He was a paragon of virtue, our standard of character, our measure of integrity, our yardstick of honor."

Judge McCall was president of the Baptist General Convention of Texas in 1964 and 1965, first vice-president of the Southern Baptist Convention from 1978 to 1980, and taught Sunday school at Waco's First Baptist Church for forty-five years.

Less than two months before his death, a resolution was introduced in the Texas Legislature by Rep. Bob Hunter, asking his colleagues to join him in recognizing McCall as "one of the great Texans in our state and one who has a great heritage." The resolution went on to cite an "unequaled record of personal and professional contributions to his church, community, city, and state that have made this notable gentleman a treasured asset."

No small thanks to Abner McCall, Baylor Law School—besides teaching good law in a small surrounding—allowed students to go to the courthouse the first day out of law school and practice law, whereas it took some graduates of other schools a little longer to acclimatize themselves to the profession.

Many Baylor lawyers have served in public service and volunteer organizations—some of the notables in state government are Mark White, Jim Mattox, Ann Richards, and Bob Bullock.

Much of that had to be due to the influence of Abner McCall, of whom Dr. Robert Sloan said, "The qualities of his life which I shall always recall are his utter honesty, his accessibility, and his open spirit."

Judge McCall had even worked for the FBI before he came back to Baylor as a professor.

He was in his early forties by the time I started there, and he was the professor of evidence and began to teach some ethics.

But he proved he'd go the extra mile for a friend in 1971.

Friends had talked me into campaigning for one of the posts of international director of Lions, and they had an appreciation/kick-off dinner for me in San Angelo, and Judge McCall made the keynote speech. It was quite an honor for me—and Judge McCall wasn't even a Lion. But Baylor was still a fairly small school, and he stood for the same things I stood for and was a great believer in volunteerism. He was also the one who talked to me about de Tocqueville, the Frenchman who came to America more than a century ago and praised the American people, saying Americans were a peculiar people because they would see the needs of others and try to meet those needs without waiting for any government—just people helping other people on their own.

Judge McCall impressed me but not only with his stature—he was physically imposing, about six-foot-three, and he had a way of throwing his fingers out to illustrate a point, so you could almost feel the information coming out at you. His lectures were magical, full of a great grasp of the bounds of common sense and law. A most intelligent man, he was very humble, but he was able to express himself in such a manner that you understood.

He was that marvel of a teacher and a legal mind—the kind who could take a topic and refine it to the point that it could be taught, but always in such a practical manner, not from the standpoint of judicious eminence. He was exacting, but always understandable. He made law that way and made life that way, teaching how to live life at the same time.

To paraphrase the prayer of Dr. Sloan—formerly of Abilene and later president of Baylor—he said: Oh, Lord, at the end of my life, whether I'm in office or out of office, make me a man who, because of his character, because of his commitment to his family and to his Savior, is as beloved as Abner McCall.

David M. Guin, Baylor law professor, recalled: "We respected him because of his character, the courage of his convictions, his unimpeachable integrity, his loyalty.

Those three—both of the Judges and my mother—would serve as great examples for anyone interested in leadership and life.

And it is just such home-grown models I have in mind as I

hope to share a lifetime's observations of leadership around the world.

But Baylor still seems to be in the good hands of those such as: Angus McSwain, one of my professors, later dean of the law school and now part time professor; Ed Horner, the fastest speaking of all professors, another law professor, who visited all 254 counties in the state of Texas and took pictures of them and had a great interest and a remarkable mind in remembering everybody that came through the law school; Dean Brad Toben of the law school who has had a great tenure and has been the guiding force in the building of one of the greatest law schools on the Brazos River that could exist; and Dr. Robert Sloan, president of the university, who has assumed the duties of president of the university and is striving to make Baylor one of the top fifty schools in the nation.

Mr. McSwain said repeatedly that the 1951 freshman class was one of the best freshman classes that he had seen. One of the reasons had to be the influx of the veterans from World War II who finished their education after the war and were entering Baylor Law School for the first time. Therefore, we had the mixture of the veterans of war and life and the young twenty- and twenty-one-year-olds seeking to better themselves through the law. I do remember that Roy Brock and Jim Dilworth were two of these veterans, who had an outstanding legal career thereafter. My group included, among others, Will Davis who distinguished himself in politics and government and was involved in every issue that arose in the insurance industry the next forty years or so in his private practice with his uncle W. W. Heath. He was most distinguished because of his service on the school board in Austin as president of the Austin school board, as state president and national president of the Association of School Boards, and then as one who served some fourteen or fifteen years as one of the appointed (and thereafter elected) members of the State Board of Education. Will has a supportive family, including Ann, who we first met while we were in law school. She also went to Baylor. Then Lisa (who married a Davis—no changes in names) had to be one of my young, favorite friends who I had the most contact with and who has been an inspiration to me by her approach to life under difficult circumstances.

Then there was Lynn, housewife and mother, and Will, Jr., minister of a large non-denominational church he founded in Austin. What a great family. Others that were involved were: Jim Price from Fort Worth, who was also a family friend of Jay; P. M. Johnston, who later became mayor of Waco along with Bob Sheehy who also was mayor of Waco; Robert "Atom Bomb" Templeton and his wife Martha, who have lived in Amarillo and Bob has been one of the top trial lawyers for the entire panhandle and state; Mike Lee—we crossed paths in the CIC and then he practiced in Abilene before moving to Fort Worth; Brad Corrigan, my good friend and study partner. And Tom Horn— a writer, drama major, and lawyer.

Chapter 5

Just the Guy in Front?

It sometimes seems as if I've been on the road since that first trip from Abilene to Maverick when I was three months old in 1931.

I've been a student of leadership almost as long, from my earliest memories of Mother and the Judge going about their daily lives in Maverick and Ballinger while trying to make things better for everybody around them.

I had other generous and exemplary leaders in my Lions career. And I've always been a little surprised to hear myself referred to as a leader, because I always had so much help it seemed like I was just the guy in front of the crowd when things happened.

There have been so many individuals who enriched my life and my career, including—but not limited to—the likes of Will Davis, who was my roommate in law school and president of the student body. He later exhibited leadership as an insurance lawyer and as a lawyer in Austin in many capacities with the Democratic Party.

Herb Petry was a lawyer-statesman, past president of Lions Club International—and the youngest president when he took office—and the record will probably never be surpassed. He was chairman of the Texas Highway Commission longer than any other individual, a true statesman and politician, both in Lions politics and state politics. He attended law school with such notables as Lloyd Bentsen and John Connally.

E. B. (Tex) Mayer was a businessman and rancher from La Grange, Texas, my closest friend, past international director of Lions Club International, a true confidante and one of the most loyal individuals I've ever known.

I always thought Tex would run for president of the Lions Clubs International as he was certainly qualified and was financially independent, but he told me at the state convention in 1974 in Waco that he was not going to run and that he would support me and work for me whole-heartedly. From that time to my presidency, he was my right-hand man and was one of the foremost politicians and organizers of clubs in Texas and Lions Clubs International. His wife Nell was beside Jay and me in every move, as well as was their son, Dr. Don Mayer, an orthodontist in LaGrange and appointee to the board by President Rohit Mecta from India. Don Mayer, a member of the Texas Longhorn fan club at the University of Texas, and Tex Mayer, an avid graduate of Texas A&M, might have both been surprised when Matthew Mayer became a member of the Baylor band where he attended school as a freshman. Tex was able to organize clubs in every mall and byway, from Austin to Houston and otherwise, and did so and helped Lionism grow in the late seventies and early eighties to its greatest heights.

Roy Minear and Carl Hyde of Midland, who were past district governors, were the two people most responsible for all my election efforts to international directorship in 1972 at Mexico City. I can never thank them enough for their generous support both financially and individually.

I would like to recognize Homer Hodge and his brother Argene. Homer Hodge of Winters is a businessman who was totally unique in his design of materials. He and Floy were totally committed to all of our campaigns during 1971-1983. They were just sixteen miles away but were totally loyal in all respects. Homer and Paul Palmer from Early, near Brownwood, are the examples of true, unselfish servants. Homer was the organizer of the Acuna Clinic, a project of our district and also the district of

Mexico and is now serving as an officer of the Crippled Children's Camp, and his wife, Dale, is a district director of the camp. All the committed and dedicated past district governors of my district deserve my undying thanks.

Past district governor and board appointee Art Cook of Lubbock wholeheartedly gave himself and his resources in Lubbock in my campaign for third vice president. Art had to be one of the most outstanding individuals and Lion member that I have ever known. He was faithful to his church, the First Baptist Church of Lubbock, to his family, to his community, to the Lubbock Downtown Lions Club, and Lions Club International. Lubbock Downtown Lions Club has been the largest or nearly the largest Lions club in our association for years, ranging from almost 300-550 members who do much to serve their community. In addition to their local contributions, they have given $75,000 for the original swimming pool at the Crippled Children's Camp and now have given another $75,000 for the expansion of the camp along with Lions Club Inernational Foundation. A great deal of their success can be directly attributed to the unselfish service of Art Cook and Jody. Art brought this same type of leadership to the board when I was able to appoint two past district governors in my years as president. It was a stroke of luck for me and the board of directors as he used his expertise on the membership committee and the service activities from the Lions Club International. In fact, the Lubbock Lions raised $75,000 in their annual 12-hour pancake feast.

And one of those I want to be sure to include in the top round of leadership abilities is Roy Schaetzel, who was general counsel for Lions Club International when I was an international director from 1972 to 1974, at the time when I was chairman of the constitution and by-laws committee. He later became executive administrator and was in that capacity while I was an officer and president and past president of Lions International.

He was a man who not only had a logical approach but had a great depth of understanding of all facets of every issue— whether it was on a local, national, or international basis. He was not only a man of legal intelligence, but a person, along with his wife Pat, of great values and a great Christian without being showy. There was no question that by his words and his actions he had deep-rooted convictions.

His associates were wonderful: Laura Heine, the most efficient secretary of Roy Schaetzel; Carole Clemens Liberti, who arranged all of the travels and was most highly efficient with the officers and entire staff; John Stewart, who aided both of our programs through his division and on into the grass roots of district and life; Donna Beckett, who was involved in our main programs and service activities. There was also June Stricat, convention coordinator; Rosemary Ozga, my secretary who is now in the youth division; Pat Cannon, public relations manager; and Robert Kleinfelder (who came to Ballinger in 1982 and was generous in his views of my work and my family), senior editor of "The Lion."

Schaetzel may well have been more responsible than anyone else for whatever success I had as a director and later president of Lions Club International.

While I was an international director, Roy and I, along with his secretary at the time, completely revised the policy manual and also indexed it for the first time—which was quite a chore but one that has saved countless hours for people looking for particular policy sections.

Also, while I was second vice-president and started thinking about my future years as president and the programs involved, I had many conferences with Schaetzel—particularly about the diabetic program and the drug program I wanted to make my major projects.

Roy knew from past experience there tended to be some wasted time for a new president because his programs were not introduced until he took office. As well, it takes some six months for a new program to work through the procedures of committees and the board and into staff implementation and on down to the local club.

Roy and I agreed it was better for maximum effectiveness to focus on one or two programs and get something going on them before taking the presidential reins.

So I introduced the drug awareness and drug-prevention program and the diabetes project to the committee of the board a year or so before I took office as president; the theory of the programs was in place, the supporting material was ready, and we were able to get the ball rolling with the district governors at the convention in Atlanta. As a result, we were successful in implementing the programs worldwide. As far as I know, Roy and I were the only two who ever saw that element and made use of it.

Later, I was able to show the directors some approaches first-hand, because we had a board meeting in Houston and San Antonio—a split meeting (the only one I knew of), but one that gave the directors a big taste of Texas—not only the big city Houston and the rodeo but also the downtown river area of San Antonio and surrounding areas including the New Braunfels Wurstfest (they organized a mini Wurstfest just for us) and we also went by the LBJ ranch on the trip from Houston to San Antonio and even stopped at the Dairy Mart in La Grange (from which along with his famous consolidated smokehouse Tex Mayer was always taking German summer sausage and tender-loin to all board meetings to give directors a taste of Texas).

And there were many other individuals who were inspirations to me for what they stood for, what they were personally, and what they encouraged others to be.

Zig Ziglar comes to mind because I first heard him speak in the late seventies, listened to his tapes, and read his books—all full of his zest for life and his eagerness to pass it on to anyone who would read or listen.

In fact, I believe it was in one of his presentations that I first found the best two-letter-ten-word speech that can be made:

"If it is to be, it is up to me."

I ended my incoming speech at Atlanta with those words, and they obviously traveled the globe as I often heard people repeating them to me in my travels.

I realized from that first speech under the old eagle on the stage of Abilene High School that I could use some help with my speaking, and I was fortunate to find help over the years from the likes of specialists.

Kay Baker of Austin, a professional speaker, worked with me on many occasions throughout the years and helped me develop a speaking style—and mainly a substantive content—to present to all types of audiences, whether professional groups,

Lions, church groups, or others. She gave me encouragement and direction through some very difficult times.

Juanell Teague of Dallas—a student of the Zig Ziglar program—worked with me on developing a brochure and such meaningful values as "Journey for Life" and adapting materials from my many travels for business audiences.

Don Reynolds, my mentor from the North Texas Speakers Association and an investment specialist, was most useful in helping this small-town West Texan to better understand the stock market and world business cycles. Don has spoken all over the world on business trends and economic forecasts.

There is simply not a way to list all of the activities of Lions Clubs International. In addition to International Programs in some 185 countries in geographical locations in the world and over 44,000 Lions clubs, unquestionably it is the largest service organization in the world. There are activities of each local Lions club that are performed for the benefit of their community, their area, and their districts (there being over 700 district governors in the world) and each of these districts has probably from fifteen to 100 clubs.

Of course, there has been mention made of some of the international projects, but in each state or country there are additional projects along with the club projects. It would be impossible to list all of the projects, but I feel that some of the projects should be listed such as:

Texas Lions Crippled Children Camp at Kerrville;
Canine Vision of Canada;
Leader Dog Michigan;
World Service of Arkansas;
Projects of the Leos;
hospitals for various causes;
research for eye, diabetes, etc.;
environmental programs;
United Nations;
Sight First Project, which raised $175 million; in addition, for many fantastic projects throughout Lionism, including the United States of America and Canada, the funding of the pro-

gram was led by Past International President Brian Stevenson of Calgary;

Youth Services/Drug Awareness;

Community Services;

Diabetes Awareness;

International Relations;

Health Services (for example, just one district of the over 700 on the submission of worldwide reports) provided an average of 1,326 voluntary service hours which worldwide would represent 59,452,536 hours of community service;

In addition, Lions Clubs annually donate an average of $20,045.00 each to charitable causes, which represents $898,737,620 in direct support to community and humanitarian needs. Lions International Foundation, which really took off in 1974 when we changed the charter at the convention in Miami, has granted more than $196.3 million for worthy projects in communities worldwide; donations last year were $19.3 million, and $21.7 million was approved in LCIF grants. At the Club Deleon International Acuna-Amistad, a project by my District 2-A1 headed by Past District Governor Paul Palmer reported in six months during 1999 there were twenty-three cataract surgeries and over 1,000 eye examinations. A Lions Club member's roar has echoed across nearly 2,000 miles to the tune of $15,000. That's the amount donated to Ballinger Memorial Hospital in one week by a Lions Club member in Maryland who asked to remain anonymous. I said, "There was a Lion in Maryland who saw something on television about the plight of hospitals in Texas. Ballinger was mentioned in the story." The anonymous donor contacted former hospital board member Rodney Flanagan on December 16. "He said he always did something at the end of the year to benefit a worthwhile cause." The donor was a friend of a man I had befriended. He had worked with me when I served as International Lions Club President a few years ago. The television program and the friendship forged through Lions Club membership were a combination which prompted the Maryland donor to make the contribution to the local hospital. "It's good for Ballinger, it's good for the hospital and it's good for Lionism," I said about the donation, "The donation is

representative of what Lionism is all about as a club and as individuals."

Sight First action plan for China pledged $15.3 million to
Lions of Hong Kong and Macau to work with the Chinese min-
istry on a five-year Blindness Prevention Program; in the first
two years of the project 910,000 cataract surgeries were performed, 92 eye care teams were dispatched to remote provinces,
2,380 opthalmologists, and 2,491 paramedics have received additional training; now the first two Lions Clubs have been organized and chartered in Mainland China.

Any type of disaster is usually met by the state or district
and/or international organization. Some of the recent examples
are:

A. $160,000.00 to Fargo, North Dakota;

B. Aid to the tornado victims in San Angelo and
Sweetwater, Texas;

C. $50,000.00 for the eye clinic in Acuna;

D. Aid to the Jarrell tornado victims;

E. $28,000.00 to the eye bank in San Angelo;

F. Recycling centers in Midland, Texas, (they had shipped
over 300,000 glasses during part of the year and are structured
to ship around 1,000,000 glasses a year) and many other places
around the states;

G. $75,000.00 grant to the Crippled Children's Camp pool
in Kerrville;

Recent eye care has been ably noted by Dear Abby articles
syndicated around the world and Bob Greene in his column of
November 6, 1996.

My dad always said our name is so important to protect, but
in another sense we do not know the reason because to us our
name seems very simple. Approximately 80% of the messages
that I leave for someone else or at the time that I make
the initial call, there is always a question as to how to spell my
name. We have heard many versions—Grindstone, Grinstaff,
Millwheel, and of course one of the most infamous came from
the lawyer that served on the state bar of directors, Richard
Haynes, who was better known as "Racehorse," which I believe
came from his track days in high school. Everyone called him

"Racehorse," and he became more famous in later years as one of the top criminal defense lawyers for several people, most notable being Cullen Davis. However, at the time of our service together, we were playing golf at a course in Dallas and during that activity "Racehorse" kept asking me, "Now, what is your name?" I think that I finally mentioned something about Grindstone, and he said, "Well, I tell you what, I think that I'm just going to call you something I can remember, *Crankshaft.*" Therefore, we can just add "Crankshaft" to the other names mentioned above, and he did call me "Crankshaft" as did a few of the other lawyers who heard him make that statement. One of the more famous name quotes was from Herb Caen, who was the morning line editor for the *San Francisco Chronicle*. In his column of May 27, 1983, this quote appeared, ". . . Lurching on: Edwin Oviaft III of First Sutter Financial here has been in correspondence with the Ballinger, Texas, law firm of Grindstaff, Grindstaff, and Slimp, and challenges anyone to top that. Even our own Low, Ball & Lynch comes in a poor second . . ." The mail still amazes me as we have had "Grindstall, Grindfall, and Limp" and all other such combinations. However, as long as they used us as lawyers or sent us business, we did not mind.

Chapter 6

ABC's from VIP's

I learned something about leadership from sheep, with which I've dealt all my life. And even though some people think they're dirty and scroungy and dumb, early on I learned the lesson in trying to assemble sheep: if you can ever get that one sheep to take the initiative to go through the gate, the others will follow (at least most of the time).

And in the process, they do a little jump as they go through the gate. In fact, during these times you can put a bar over the gate and the sheep will jump over it and continue to go through. If you're nimble enough, you can remove the bar, but the sheep will still jump as if they were jumping over the bar. This is an example of animal leadership.

During my years on the international board of the Lions—and particularly the year I was international president—I had countless opportunities to see leadership at work, in many languages, for all shades of skin, for religious persuasions of which I'd seldom if ever heard, and in all stations of life.

And I've seen leaders in all kinds of clothes, from uniforms and crowns and robes to skirts and bathing suits.

I now suppose I paid attention to leadership in others because I knew, deep down, I was no more leadership material than the guy in front of the next cotton sack, and I wanted to pay close attention to the qualities of leaders to see if I might be able to adapt some of them to my own situation. I really didn't have a lot of choice as a kid, because sitting idly in a corner around my folks would have been like not breathing.

Now, after more than half a century of leadership watching, I'm trying to capture those qualities in my own mind and get them on paper for others who are inspired and sometimes in awe of those who step forward and say, or imply, "Follow me . . ."

There doesn't seem to be an overwhelming geographical quotient to leadership—although I tend to agree with de Tocqueville that the United States probably produces more grassroot leaders simply because Americans have that unusual knack for stepping in to get things done wherever they see something that needs doing and nobody else doing it at the moment.

My passport—and recollections—indicate I've met national and governmental leaders in Casablanca, Bangkok, Karachi and Pakistan, Seoul, Helsinki, Kuala Lumpur, Stockholm, Taipei, Vienna, Tokyo, Madrid, Canberra, Australia, Lisbon, Cairo, Wellington, Harare, Zambia, Singapore, Johannesberg, Sri Lanka, Asuncion, New Delhi, Santiago, London, Buenos Aires, Istanbul, West Berlin, Paris, Jerusalem, Mexico City, New York and Washington, D. C.—and a lot of other places that don't come to mind at the moment.

The two biggest surprises were usually how different the leaders looked—and how much they seemed to think alike.

I don't talk a lot about differences in religion, because I think that is a very personal matter, but I think at least something you might like to call "spirituality" accounts for a lot of leadership, and it answered a lifelong suspicion for me when I came across a list of the great spiritual thinkers and their commitment to what we've come to know as "The Golden Rule."

The Christian version, cited in Matthew 7:12 of the New Testament and dating to about 30 AD, is the most familiar in this country: "Therefore, all things whatsoever you desire that men should do to you, do you even to them. For this is the Law and the prophets."

But Confucius was quoted some 500 years earlier: "Surely

it is the maxim of loving kindness, do not unto others that which you would not have them do unto you."

The Judaic code from the Talmud, some 1300 years B.C. reads: "What is hateful to you, do not to your fellow man. That is the entire Law, all the rest is commentary."

The Hindus put it this way in prehistoric times: "This is the sum of duty. Do not unto others that which would cause you pain if done unto you."

The Zoroastrian saying, about 600 B.C., was: "That nature alone is good which refrains from doing unto another whatsoever is not good for itself."

The Islam rule from the Koran, about 600 B.C., noted: "No one of you is a believer until he desires for his brother that which he desires for himself."

The Buddhist belief, dating to about 525 B.C. is: "Hurt not others in ways that you find hurtful."

Socrates (470-399 B.C.) was quoted as saying: "Do not do unto others that which would anger you if others did it to you.

The teaching of Tao, about 500 B.C., was: "Regard your neighbor's gain as your gain and your neighbor's loss as your loss."

And the Sikhs noted, about 1500 A.D.: "We obtain salvation by loving our fellow man and God."

Of course, it would be difficult to pick a modern person who better exemplifies the term world leader than Pope John Paul, whom I met in Rome in 1983.

Hardly anybody in the world is busier than the pope, and Jay and I found ourselves ushered into a confined area at St. Peter's Basilica just before he was due to address a crowd of some 12,000 celebrants in the huge square outside one of the most beautiful and awe-inspiring buildings in the world.

Regardless of church membership, one has to be impressed with the pope, and Jay and I felt like barefoot children before a king as we approached the prelate. But it was on Lions Club business and the meeting was in the works, so we tried to relax. I had a silver tray to be presented from the Lions, and a little sculpture of a cowboy—which seemed a bit, well, Texan, and Jay was carrying a set of rosary beads a friend from Ballinger had asked to be blessed.

His Holiness immediately put us at ease. It seemed as if we were the only two people in the world he wanted to visit with at the moment, and he listened to my report on the Lions anti-drug and diabetes awareness programs that had been chosen as world projects for my administration. We knew he was dedicated to youth and would be interested in the diabetes and anti-drug programs. But he accepted the silver tray with gratitude and obviously loved the cowboy statue—and carefully and seriously blessed the beads for Jay's friend.

Real leadership is more interested in others than in itself, I thought, and Pope John Paul II had to be one of the most compassionate and caring people I ever met. His whole personality was radiant with love for others.

Then he went out on the balcony and showed that love to 12,000 people in eight different languages.

I'm sorry I didn't get to meet her personally, but I saw that same love and devotion at work in the late Mother Theresa when she was honored with the Lions Clubs International Humanitarian Award for her lifelong mission to the poorest of the poor. And I have often used her saintly statement: "We cannot all do great things, but we can do small things in a great way."

When I recently looked at a photograph of Jay and me with the pope, I realized I was wearing a set of presidential cufflinks given to me earlier by Ronald Reagan during a visit to the White House—which is at least the U.S. equivalent of the pope's St. Paul home.

And there were other similarities.

President Reagan was surely one of the greatest communicators since Franklin D. Roosevelt; he did with television what FDR had done with the fledgling radio half a century earlier. He made it his own—and made millions of Americans feel he was chatting with them in their living rooms.

Jay and I met the Reagans in connection with the Lions anti-drug program in 1983.

We had been invited to have lunch in the White House with Dr. Carlton Turner, who was then administrator of the White House drug abuse program for which Nancy Reagan's "Just Say No" slogan had been the hallmark.

There's a different aura about the White House than the

pope's quarters, because we Americans own it and feel a pride of proprietorship. Jay and I were made to feel a bit more at home when we ran into a friend from Winters, Texas, a dozen miles up the road from Ballinger. This friend, Love Smith, was the executive director of the Horacio Alger Foundation and a classmate of ours at Baylor.

We also ran into two fellow Texans, the late Senator John Tower and billionaire Ross Perot, who were there to share honors for Ross's son with the Freedom Flight Award.

Suddenly, as Jay and I were escorted into the Oval Office— and I was juggling a plaque for Mrs. Reagan and a western sculpture for the president—I was the barefoot boy in front of the pope again. I think I handed the gifts off to a secret service man, or to Jay, as the president approached with his hand out.

Then he said, "Come on, Nancy, they're here . . .," and it was as if we were visiting with friends across the fence at Ballinger. The most powerful man in the world was expecting us and seemed excited to see us—despite the fact that I must have been the thousandth person he'd seen that week under similar circumstances.

Here was an incredible ability to be involved with everyone on an individual basis—and, somehow, I think it was a natural instinct with Reagan, not even something he had learned before the Hollywood cameras. He was real, and he was really interested in everyone he met.

Jimmy Carter was just finishing his four-year term as president when I met him during a Lions International Convention in Atlanta in 1982. There was no time to get nervous because he and Rosalyn entered the coffee room backstage where we were all waiting to be on the program.

But talk about the guy next door. Jimmy Carter seemed to have invented the idea of neighborliness. As I was trying to talk about peanuts and world affairs, he kept bubbling up with questions about me and Jay and Ballinger and Lions projects—and you could tell he really cared.

At one point, I got up to give a seat to Mrs. Carter, but Jimmy pulled my coattail and said, "No, sit down. She can take care of herself. I want to talk to you about Lionism." He had been a Lions district governor and had attended the International Convention at Dallas in 1968, so he was thoroughly familiar with Lions Clubs and Lions Club projects.

It was no surprise to us when the ex-president and Rosalyn moved right out of the White House and into the Habitat for Humanity program—not only giving the housing program great publicity and attracting huge membership increases, but showing up with a hammer and saw at actual conferences around the world. They may have been the best good-will ambassadors that ever came out of the White House—not to mention some of the best examples of Christianity at work. At this point, Lions Clubs International has joined hands with President Carter in the Habitat for Humanity program.

Of course, I had met fellow Texan President Lyndon Johnson, and he was an impressive guy, but in a different way. Lyndon was always onstage, the consummate politician; but his concern for the poor and the uneducated—and those without electricity, in his early days—was as real as his hearty grin, his Texas charisma, and his abdominal scar.

And he no doubt suffered in comparison with the suave, boyish, and Camelot aura of the top half of his presidential ticket in 1960, but Lyndon not only held this country together through some questionable times after the assassination of John F. Kennedy but went on to change our world with his "Great Society" and "War on Poverty." And, of course, his charming and industrious widow, Lady Bird Johnson, is both a Texas treasure and an unprecedented boon to Texas wild flowers and the visual environment. Her National Wildflower Center at Johnson City will be a permanent example for good citizenship long after we're all gone.

President George Bush from Texas and president number forty-one, who is the father of George W. Bush and president number forty-three, made an impact on our governmental society for years prior to his becoming president. He served as vice president and served in China and in many different capacities of governmental service. Many of my friends in Midland knew President Bush and always touted his expertise and demeanor. We had the opportunity to see him in action in 1981 at a Lions convention in Phoenix, Arizona, as he was in charge of a "Drug Force and/or Program" for the United States and even Mexico.

He spoke on that subject at the convention and was probably the impetus needed for us to begin the drug program on an international basis.

We had the opportunity to meet with President Bush at a Lions convention in England at which time he was the principal speaker and gave a great address. He and Barbara Bush continue to have an impact on the American way of life in addition to having two sons as governors at the same time, and lastly, to have one son who serves as the current president of the United States.

They were always involved; they always made a difference.

Maybe not in quite the same rarefied category with presidents and prelates, but another vivid and world-famous VIP, Art Linkletter, impressed me with his warmth and outgoing personality when I met him at the airport in Honolulu, Hawaii.

And, not unusually, it could have been an embarrassing situation for me.

The wonderfully efficient and prescient Lions coordinators out of Chicago had arranged for me to meet Linkletter at the airport. I was returning from my world tour as international Lions president, and having made it through more than fifty countries without major blunders, I was not dissatisfied with myself—particularly since I had enough exposure in the media and in Lions events that people recognized me in the waiting area, and I had to acknowledge greetings and give informal reports to a variety of travelers who were arriving for the convention. The main group on this particular flight was a group from South America, and they were very enthusiastic about meeting their president, especially since we had just visited there. It appeared that there was a complete circle around me, and I was trying to shake hands and be the gentleman and at the same time watching out of one eye for Art Linkletter.

I missed the Linkletters in the crowd.

By the time I realized it and rushed to the plane to check with the stewardess—who confirmed that I had missed the television star—I was beginning to feel some of the old panic and embarrassment as I hurried to the baggage claim area—and found the Linkletters retrieving their own luggage like any other travelers.

I rushed over and introduced myself and began an elaborate apology when Linkletter turned on that famous thousand-watt smile and said there was no reason to apologize; he knew I had been busy, too, and he had gone on about his business of deplaning.

Again, it was leadership in action—thinking of others and working on solutions, not stewing over problems.

It was ironic that a year or so later we were in Kyoto, Japan, for a board meeting and staying in one of the elite suites, which had bulletproof glass, and they told us the suite would be occupied by President Sadat a month or two later. President Sadat was assassinated before he made that trip.

I have described meetings with President Sadat at Cairo and Prime Minister Begin in Israel, and although they were among the first big-name world leaders with whom I had brief personal experiences, they remain two shining examples of the epitome of leadership—in both their cases, to the extent of giving their lives for their goals of peace in a troubled region of the world.

Sadat's courage has been well documented in his ultimate sacrifice for peace. But I was impressed with his ability to put me and my associates at ease despite his own problems at the time.

And I'll never forget that Begin took time out to see me on my Lions Club mission despite the fact that he'd just come from a meeting of his cabinet after Iraq had attacked Iran overnight. I later read with great interest the biography he gave me at the time, but I was not surprised to read of his devotion to the democratic way of life and his struggles to defend his homeland in command of the Irgun.

I had seen it in his composure, his steely gaze, and his firm handshake: he was a leader among leaders.

Much more recently, I had occasion to remember Jacques Chirac, who I met years ago when he was the mayor of Paris, one of the world's largest cities. As of this writing, he is the president of France and a leader in European and global affairs.

Those were, admittedly, some of the more spectacular leaders I have had the honor and pleasure to meet personally, but I could go on and on recalling leaders great and small from countries great and small with whose attitudes and abilities I was impressed. For now, it should be useful to try to itemize some of the characteristics I saw in such leaders that may be adapted to leaders of today and tomorrow:

1. They were not afraid—or too busy—to be individually involved;
2. they accepted responsibility;
3. they made a difference;
4. they were ethically tough;
5. they were team builders, not ego builders;
6. they were good organizers of time;
7. and they practiced the Golden Rule—by whatever name they knew it.

Part Two

Putting It into Practice

Can you make a difference? I believe you can.

If you would imagine with me the most beautiful beach in the world: white sand, rocks at one end of the beach, palm trees at the other end, and blue-green clear water that would rush to the rocks and the water crystals that would spring up from there, and the additional beauty on that beach. Onto the end of the beach comes an older man—stooped shoulders, decrepit in age, wrinkled face with long white hair; and he is leaning over and picking up one of the many hundreds of starfish and throwing it in the water; then moving to the next starfish and repeating the process—all the way down to the palm trees at the other end.

Then along comes a young boy—probably twelve to fourteen years of age—from the palm tree end, and he is watching the old man pick up the starfish and toss them into the water. He stops the old man and says, "Hey, old man, what are you doing?"

"Well, I'm moving these starfish from the beach to the water," the old man answers. Then the boy says "Old man, there are hundreds and thousands of starfish on the beach. You can't make any difference."

The old man looked to the young boy but without a word.

52

Then he leaned over and picked up a starfish and threw it into the water. Then he turned to the young man and said, "It made a difference to that one."

Yes, you can make a difference.

Introduction to Part Two

The first part of this book has been mostly autobiographical, attempting to familiarize readers with my background, my people, my career in Lionism, and travels around the world and around my mind in search of the leadership and service that have been the focus of this book and, I hope, most of my life.

But that's really just the beginning: my life and careers in Lionism and the law for whatever examples—good and not so good—they have suggested.

At least as important to the reader may be various gleanings from friends and associates and community, national, and world leaders from whom I have learned more than I will ever be able to pass on.

But, while such insights may be important in individual and world affairs, they don't always lend themselves to handy categorizing.

So I have considered many of them together in this section under six chapter heads, plus half a dozen columns I wrote for the West Texas newspaper *The Abilene Reporter-News,* and my inaugural speech when I assumed the weighty position as president of Lions International. It may be interesting to compare my attitudes and statements more than two decades ago with some of the later material.

Wherever possible, I have attributed these concepts, ideas, experiences, and outright quotations to their sources, but many of them are the kind of community property that produces sayings, anecdotes, truisms, and the like.

And, because communication is at least one of the most important and often most nerve-wracking skills of leadership, I have written a separate chapter with some suggestions on formulating, writing, and delivering an effectual speech for your club, community, or larger-focus group.

Which, again, is not to claim any great expertise or ability as a public speaker. My style is probably classified as colloquial, at best, and my utterances—usually among colleagues of Lionism or the law—have been intended mostly to share whatever information I happened to have at the moment with as little showiness as possible. Dad always told me to be kind but yet firm and honest.

At any rate, I have made literally thousands of speeches without being run off a stage or having any serious missiles thrown at me.

After you know simple facts of my life, this latter section of the book is likely to be the part most often revisited for ideas, inspiration, company, or comparative satisfaction during your own trip crossing whatever Sinais you encounter.

Read it in good health, and remember that you are the final authority on what parts may apply to you and what you may wish to do about them. But this I am certain of, that you—any of you—can make a difference.

Chapter 7

Integrity and Ethics: Do We Have Enough of Either?

I-N-T-E-G-R-I-T-Y. Yes, integrity.

It takes courage, and courage is really honesty. People who are operating with real courage are actually exhibiting integrity. They have to do what they are doing or they will be disloyal. Our dreams are entrusted to our care with the obligation to turn ideas into creative action. As an honest trustee, you will be so motivated by integrity that you will have no place for fear.

As a child, I used to go to my grandfather's dairy and truck farm near Abilene, Texas. It was hot, it had the sandiest soil in the world, and he raised watermelons and cantaloupes as well as cows. Of course, the cows had to be milked every morning and every night without a single exception; and of course, I had the pleasure to join into this venture, which at a very young age was a delight. As I got a little older, it became more of a chore, but my grandfather always said come hell or high water those cows had to be milked, and it was always my chore to help milk—and that was long before small dairies had automatic milking equipment. But I'm still a little proud that no problem ever got in the way of what I had to do.

In later years, that included delivering milk—as well as melons and other farm produce—to the many small grocery stores along Abilene's Pine and Grape streets. Dealing with grocers is a different kind of training from dealing with milk cows.

A different kind of training—and certainly more difficult and with less compassionate teachers than my grandparents—came when I was hired to carry water to the carpenters during the building of Ballinger's Bruce Field in the second World War. I was eleven or twelve then.

Later, I was hired to help kill mesquite with kerosene. I drove fifteen miles out in the country to find that the other workers—all of them older—had left me the biggest can. The other cans were three-gallon cans, but I was left with a five-gallon monster. I carried it around for three days—just barely able to hold it, and sloshing kerosene down my leg with every step. The first day when I went home I was blistered through my blue jeans.

After three days on that ranch, we were to move to another ranch on the following Monday morning. They gave me the directions, and when I got there they admitted they had bets on whether or not I would show up.

After that I had no problems with my co-workers.

You can call that responsibility, you can call it accountability, but it adds up to integrity, and integrity leaves little room for fear or being too tired.

In recent years many people have been turning their backs on the basic moral values, and we are paying a terrible price for this. Scandals have tarnished reputations from banking and savings and loans to the capitols in Austin and Washington and the pulpits of television ministries and have affected each of us in some phase of life.

The American people must begin demanding high ethical standards from their leaders in politics, business, and religion, but the public must also make a commitment to those ethics.

Fred Wertheimer, the head of the government pressure group Common Cause made this statement in December of 1989: "This has not been a good decade for values. I really believe that we are about to change on that. I think the pendulum is swinging." That is encouraging, and because of my opportunities for travels throughout the world, I see the same pendulum swinging on ethical standards and personal lives—business and professional lives—and there is no question in my mind that a new emphasis will be placed on home and marriage, and once again the family unity will become the cornerstone of our nation.

But please don't think integrity—and its absence in public affairs—is a new phenomenon.

One of the wonders of the world is the Great Wall of China that extends for more than two thousand miles along the border between Mongolia and China. It was built in the third century before Christ by the emperor Shi Huang Ti, who used 300,000 laborers, mostly prisoners. The wall was erected twenty to fifty feet high and fifteen to twenty-five feet thick, with towers at regular intervals. And do you know that no army ever breached that wall in combat? They didn't need to. They simply bribed the gatekeepers and came through without having to force an entrance.

When the American General William Dean was captured in the Korean War, he was permitted to write one letter home. He enclosed a word to his son. What did he write? Did he say, "Son, go out and make a lot of money"? Did he say, "Son, I hope you do this or do that"? No. He said, "Bill, remember that integrity is the most important thing of all. Let it always be your aim."

Integrity is the glue that holds our way of life together. What our young people want to see in their elders is integrity, honesty, truthfulness, and faith. What they hate the most is hypocrisy and phoniness.

There is a possibility that a new wave of moral and spiritual conviction will touch a rising generation, and if a new moral climate sweeps this nation, Americans will rebel against the growing sex, violence, and filth on T.V., bringing back some old-fashioned, clean family entertainment.

Yes, a new spirituality is upon us as related by Dr. Billy Graham and the best-selling book in the world which has never been surpassed. The Bible shall again be the book that we will turn to for guidance and inspiration and for those basic values. Those values are all in that book and by far the majority of all of the self-help, self-improvement, self-image ideas all tie back to the teachings of the Bible.

Americans have gone through wars and pestilence and survived, and because of the possible impact of the latest revolution of the Iron Curtain countries, we have the best possibility for peace and individuals being involved in the restoration of the basic values of life throughout the world.

In late June of 1989, I had the opportunity to speak to an individual from Hungary who was attending an international Lions convention in Miami.

(In 1988 Lions Clubs International for the first time organized clubs in Hungary, Poland, and Estonia. Prior to that time, one of the requirements for the organization of a club in any country in the world was that the individual have the basic choice to join if that is his desire. Six clubs were organized in Hungary, and as a result, the district governor or representative of these clubs was able to attend the international convention in Miami.)

The Hungarian I met was in a group of 1,400 to whom I had the opportunity to make a presentation, and I had a further conversation with him at a reception that evening. Lazslo Czegledi was a lawyer from Budapest, and he told me this freedom of choice was absolutely the greatest thing that ever happened to him and his country in his lifetime. Not only was he enthusiastic about life, he had hope for the future.

Americans do not realize the importance of this basic value of freedom, although we are a strong people with a pioneering spirit and a heritage of faith in God. I feel that we never had a stronger faith in the American spirit in the same sense as related by Tom Safford, the astronaut who commanded the final Apollo Six as well as Apollo Ten and likened the mission to the "conquering of the west, the epitome of the great American spirit."

Since the Old Testament days, integrity has been something sought after, difficult to accomplish, but yet a value that is restrictive. It was said that David shepherded according to the integrity in his heart. Do you act according to integrity? If so, when you give your work, you do so exactly as you say you would because integrity means that you are verbally trustworthy. Furthermore, when bills come due you pay them, because integrity means that you are financially dependable. You don't fudge because you are able to cover your tracks; neither do you fake it because you are now a big shot. Being successful doesn't give anybody the right to call wrong right or to say something is O.K. if it isn't O.K.

How Does Integrity Relate to Ethics?

We do give a lot of lip-service to the word integrity, and most of us agree it is much needed in today's society. In December 1989, I had a discussion to define the word ethics with one word. My answer was "value," or the value of integrity.

Kenneth Blanchard and Dr. Norman Vincent Peale wrote a fine book concerning ethics and suggested an ethics check which consists of three questions. (Now let's stop right here and realize that when we talk about any of these principles, any of these values, or any of this involvement, we are talking about something that applies to personal, family, and business affairs.) Their ethics check consisted of three questions:

1. Is it legal?
2. Is it balanced? (That is, is the decision going to be fair, or will it heavily favor one party over another in the short or long term?)
3. How will it make me feel about myself?

The legal question gets you to look at existing standards.

The balance question activates your sense of fairness and rationality.

The last question focuses on your emotions and your own standards of morality.

I gave a speech in 1991 at Angelo State University on "Marriage and Family Therapy" and talked about the future. I asked the audience, "Which of these inventions do you think we could see in the twenty-first century: (A) a hypersonic plane that takes you from New York to Tokyo in less than three hours; (B) a magnetically levitated train that travels 300 miles an hour; (C) a voice-activated wristwatch computer that simultaneously translates from English to any foreign language; (D) a pill that can temporarily increase your memory by four hundred percent, (E) pigs the size of cows, cows as big as elephants, and even genetically altered human beings, or (F) all of the above?"

If you answered all of the above, you're right on the money. And, what's more, we're not talking about the year 2100. This amazing technology has affected us or will begin to affect us within the next twenty years, according to Don C. Reynolds, investment counselor for Smith-Barney and an educator and worldwide speaker and a mentor of mine from the North Texas Speakers Association.

I realize many non-Texans can't appreciate the proportions of my native land. Many are shocked to learn that Ballinger is about 450 miles from El Paso. But everything Texan isn't big. Ballinger itself, I tell people, is about 5,000 people—on a Saturday night. And for entertainment we used to go down to the theater and watch the corn pop or go to the Safeway store and watch them unload. And the bigger guys liked to go down to the Greyhound bus station and watch the dog get off the bus to tinkle.

We have a new traffic light, and the Chamber of Commerce is going to decide the color. We don't have a United Fund; we just exchange gifts.

But my ancestors came from eastern Tennessee, where we recently attended a convention and were praising the interstate highway system. We were told about the older couple driving on the freeway and seeing a sign that said "Eat X-Lax and stay young." So they got off the highway and found a store and got some X-Lax.

Soon after they resumed their trip they saw another X-Lax sign, so they got off the main road and found some X-Lax and took it to stay young. This happened several times before the husband leaned over to his wife and reported, "I've just done a childish thing. . . ."

Are We Sweeping Ethics Under the Rug?

The late Senator Margaret Chase Smith (R-Maine) once decried what had happened to the word "square" in her lifetime.

"Many years ago the word 'square' was one of the most honored words in our vocabulary," she said. "The square deal was an honest deal. A square meal was a full and good meal. It was the square shooter rather than the sharp-shooter who was admired."

"What is square today? He's the fellow who never learned to get away with it, who gets choked up when the flag unfurls. There has been too much glorification of the angle players, the corner cutters, and the goof-offs," Senator Smith noted. "One of America's greatest needs is for more people who are square."

Do we need more square individuals or are we content in sweeping ethics under the rug? To answer this important question and to determine whether we are cut out for the new century, we must ask ourselves the following:

1. Is ethics fashionable?
2. Do I take ethics seriously?
3. Do I understand ethical conduct?

We have apparently escaped the nuclear destruction of earth but real dangers are lurking in the 2000s, and it may be more dangerous for Americans than any other decade in our memory. We face threats from an attack of legal germs and poisonous gas. We will suffer the woes of drug abuse for generations. Hate groups abound. But what disturbs me the most is the antagonism and conflict among Americans. The absence of ethics is fashionable, but it is present in political offices, campaign contributions, governmental positions, savings and loan associations, college athletic programs, local government positions (city, county and school), religion, TV ministries, vocations, and professions.

The concept of ethics has been fashionable for thousands of years, and it is and should be one of the most timely subjects on the threshold decade of the twenty-first century. Even though we are sitting in the front seat of one of the most exhilarating and exciting decades in the century, it appears we do not know the meaning of ethics, nor do we know the application of ethics in our everyday life.

There is no question that we live in a global world (Bejing Kentucky Fried Chicken, Moscow McDonald's, Tokyo Domino's Pizza). We can have breakfast in Paris, dinner in Hong Kong—and yet our baggage is still at Ft. Worth-Dallas airport. Even though it might be a slight exaggeration, it has been said we will soon be able to board a flight around the world that will take only an hour, but it will take over an hour to get to the airport.

Even ethics is a global word as it comes from the Greek work "ethos" for character. Plato and Aristotle thought ethical conduct was virtuous conduct and that the practice of virtuous conduct would build character. *Harvard Business Review* defines ethics as a set of moral principles or values to guide behavior; and ethical behavior conforms to these moral principles and basic principles. Maybe the simplest definition is: "values we use to distinguish right from wrong."

Because of the fast technology and scientific changes that have been made, soon the two-way video wristwatches which first appeared in the comics of Dick Tracy will be a reality, and now a laser has been developed which can cut through the hard core of a diamond but at the same time can intricately weld together the retina of an eye. However, if we shift to the development of stable human relationships, we need to analyze our attitude in our treatment of our fellow man. Is that attitude summarized in the memo of Lincoln Savings and Loan Branch: "Capitalize on this—always remember the weak, meek and ignorant are always good targets."

Lawyers Need Ethics Too

But folks around Ballinger who recall that I have practiced law for some half a century are likely to ask: "What about your own profession?"

And what is the image of the lawyer as far as the public is concerned?

A recent poll of 7,000 families by a New York research organization of fifty products and services showed that Americans think chicken and video rentals are terrific buys while hospitals and lawyers charge too much.

Peter Brown, a New York lawyer, in the book *Rascals* noted that lawyers today are greedy rascals affected by narcissism and egotism and further stated that the manners and morals of lawyers have been in steady decline. And lawyers don't respect themselves all that much, according to a survey by the *National*

Law Journal and West Publishing Company of more that 1,000 lawyers around the nation. Asked what lawyers least like about other lawyers, 56% cited obnoxiousness, 34% said conceit, 29% cited greed, and 24% decried inflexibility. But when asked what they like most about other lawyers, the most common answers were intelligence 54% and integrity 46%.

Lawyers have reason for self doubt. Less than 25% of Americans who responded to a Roper Poll expressed confidence in attorneys—down from 44% in 1978. One out of three polled—twice as many as in 1978—accused lawyers of giving clients wrong information or charging too much.

Caroline Corbin, in her book *Strategies 2000,* indicates that there will be a shift from living at the speed of light to the development of stable human relationships; but we must have a caring people—people who treat their fellow men as they would like to be treated.

Society indicates that we will not take ethics seriously until we care for other people seriously. If we are going to understand ethical conduct, people must understand what ethics means, how it can be used, how you can live ethically, and how you can teach ethics. There is one value, one core word that is the glue that holds all other values together—integrity. What is your definition?

Actually, it is fairly simple, isn't it? Is it honest? Is it truthful? Is it upright? Is it fair? Is there freedom from deceit or fraud? We have all heard the adage that honesty is the best policy, but actually honesty needs to be a way of life. There was a time when people dealt from an ethical base in their lives, but things began to change for the worse and unethical behavior became more common, even applauded. Those acting ethically or showing loyalty to an employer evoked snickers and sneers from others.

Integrity is something that must be thought of as a valuable commodity, one that no one can take away from you even in times of despair and economic difficulty. Leaders of the sales world are known as much for their personal integrity as for their sales skills, and leaders of the free world are known and remembered for their values as well. There is not a business profession or organization that is not initiating awareness in order that their entity is not tarnished. Even the Internal Revenue Service made 17,000 of its employees sit through integrity awareness briefings during 1990 and 1991. And more attention is now being given by the tax collectors to consumer issues.

Individuals are responsible for their actions to preclude such actions of an ethics committee of any business or organization. If we care, ethical conduct will be improved and our profession will be improved. Societies change only when individuals change.

There are going to be changes in society and there are going to be changes in the legal profession. Are you ready to change?

The minister, after taking over a small church, aimed his first sermon at the evils of drinking. Afterwards, one of the deacons suggested that, in the future, he steer clear of that subject because about a fourth of the church's members worked at a nearby brewery.

So, the second Sunday, the preacher lashed out at the evils of gambling. Another deacon drew him aside and informed him that about a fourth of the church's members worked at a race track.

On the third Sunday, the preacher's message was built around the evils of smoking. Still another deacon told him that about a fourth of the congregation was composed of tobacco farmers.

On the fourth Sunday, the preacher chose as his subject the evils of selling contaminated food in Denmark.

He changed.

As attorneys, our code of professional responsibility is changing. The Supreme Court has already addressed some of the ethical issues facing the legal society.

Consider these questions:

1. Is it right to prepare pleadings and interrogatories only on the basis of what is in our word processor or computer?

2. Are our fees based on the quantities of material rather than the quality of our work product?

3. Is it ethical to file volumes of interrogatories and discover that 80% of them do not apply to issues involved in that particular lawsuit?

4. Should you take a case when some other person could better serve the needs of your client? (For instance, marriage or family therapists?)

5. Should you destroy damaging documents you were obligated to produce in response to a discovery request?

6. Do we care about our employees?

7. Do we examine ourselves and make certain that we are setting an example of ethical conduct?

We have rules of conduct, we have seminars on legal ethics, but we must motivate ourselves not only to understand, not only what is ethical, but also to act in an ethical manner. If you merely glance through the basic topics of our code, you will find that integrity and honesty is the core of the entire code. It is much more satisfying to be able to say, "I did it because I ought," rather than "I did it because I was compelled."

Frankly, the figures as recited by the press seem overstated, but I am certain that that is the trend during the last thirty years. As I look back, I think about the fact that I was one director out of fifteen directors of the state bar in 1971-1974, and on that date there were approximately 20,000 lawyers and now some thirty years later there are over 65,000 lawyers; therefore, just in addition to time and way of life, the numbers would also increase to some extent because of the tripling of the numbers that have passed the bar. Furthermore, in my humble opinion, that regardless of the percentages and the professions involved that the percentage of any profession or any organization or school or family is higher than it should be and that we all need to realize the importance and take control of our own destiny or assist in taking control and put them in the image of our professional organization.

If it is really that simple, why don't more people practice and live ethical conduct in their everyday lives? Is it because:

1. they do not realize how important it is;
2. it takes tremendous self-control;
3. we do not care for other people seriously.

Most of us are concerned about how we think and how we

feel and do not pay enough attention to the thoughts and feelings of others. After all, ethics is just the moral strength to do what we know is right and to avoid doing what we know is wrong. Sometimes it's just a little common sense.

Harry Emerson Fosdick, the author of *On Being A Real Person,* in his lecture, "Six Ways to Tell Right From Wrong," says:

1. The test of common sense: Should I say to myself, 'Don't be silly.'?;

2. The test of sportsmanship: Do I propose to abide by the rules of fair play?;

3. The test of our best selves: Have I carried the decision up to my finest self?;

4. The test of publicity: What if everybody knew what I am proposing to do?;

5. The test of our most admired personality: What would he do under the circumstances?;

6. The test of foresight: Where does this course of behavior come out? I think it also helps to have a sense of humor.

Franklin Delano Roosevelt, our president from 1932 to his death in 1945, led us through the nation's worst depression and worst world war, and probably at the cost of his own health. Struck by polio as a young father, just as he was getting into the physically and emotionally grueling routine of politics, he neglected a regimen of rehabilitation that might have extended his life and his health, opting to devote himself in full to leading the country out of the throes of the depression of the 1930s and into the rigors of the world-girdling war.

And he apparently had an often devilish sense of humor. The story is told that one day he got tired of the pleasant nothings of White House receptions in which he was expected to say the same things to hundreds of people. So he decided to see if anybody was really paying attention.

For a time, when a guest took his hand he would flash the famous FDR smile and say, "I murdered my grandmother this morning." Most of the guests responded with the usual pleasantries such as "How lovely," or "Just continue with your great work."

Just as he thought, they weren't paying any attention. That is except for one foreign diplomat, who, when FDR admitted murdering his grandmother, responded softly, "I'm sure she had it coming to her."

Chapter 8

Making IRS Work for You

A woman was seeking to divorce her husband, and when the judge asked for the reasons she replied, "Well, Judge, he just won't do right, and I have nagged him and nagged him, but he just won't do right."

The judge asked her if she had tried heaping coals of fire on his head. The woman thought and said, "No, but I don't think it would help. I have tried scalding water and that did no good."

Obviously she had missed the point.

Everyone has a point of view. Yes, and sometimes even a different point of view. A pessimist sees a glass of water and says it's half empty; the optimist sees a glass of water and says it's half full.

The pessimist wakes up in the morning, opens up the windows and says, "Oh my God, morning." The optimist wakes up in the morning, opens up the windows and says, "Good morning, God."

Three men were discussing their weekend and one of them said, "Well, I wasted the weekend with my children"; the second one said, "Well, I spent the weekend with my children"; and the third one said, "Well, I invested the weekend with my children."

I share the third man's point of view, but the anecdote

Goodwill West Texas
4216 College Hills Blvd
San Angelo TX 76904
(325) 617-7911
www.goodwillwesttexas.org

SALES RECEIPT
1381
Sale Number: **********
02/26/2015 10:29:53 AM

Qty	Item Special	Price Discount
1	Socks	5.50

	Sub Total:	5.50
	Tax:	0.45
	Total:	5.95

Payment Types and Amounts:
CASH
20.00

Change Due: -14.05

All sales final. No refunds or exchanges.
DONATE STUFF. CREATE JOBS.
Thank You

demonstrates the variety to be found in points of view. I also believe the greatest investment you can make toward your success in all phases of life—personal, family, and business—is something I remember through the initials "IRS," which allows us to expand our opportunity for excellence. An old Chinese story illustrates the point by comparing a frog sitting at the bottom of a well—which thinks the sky is only as big as the rim of the well—while the frog that has surfaced has an entirely different point of view.

And don't worry; my IRS has nothing to do with taxes or any part of the bureaucracy of the federal government but simply notes:

I—individual involvement;
R—recognized values;
S—service to all.

There are two parts to individual involvement:

1. You are the key;
2. There is ample room for each of us.

The most significant example of individual esteem has to be that of grandparents with their own grandchildren. When I finally got to be a grandpa, I realized all those grandparents who talked about their grandchildren are not nearly as crazy as I thought.

But don't get yourself in the situation of the Louisiana woman whose grandson asked, "Grandmama, how old are you?" and she said, "Well, grandsons don't ask their Grandmama how old they are." The next day he asked, "Grandmama, how much do you weigh?" and the grandmother said, "Well, grandsons do not ask their grandmamas how much they weigh." And the next day he came back and said, "Grandmama, I'm not going to ask you how much you weigh and I'm not going to ask you how old you are because I found your drivers license and on the drivers license it said that you weigh 138 pounds and that you are sixty-two years old—and besides that the driver's license says you got an F in sex."

But real individuals are the key to opportunity, and you are that key, which is a tremendous responsibility. There is nobody on the face of the earth who can use your talents except you, and that is an awesome responsibility. But, listen, you are somebody—you are important even though you are one individual in a large world of some five billion people. It is individuals that count. Yes, the same individuals who create disturbances, pull triggers, and drop bombs also make discoveries, preach sermons, write editorials. One individual is often largely responsible for the defeat or victory of an entire team

If we go back into history, some of the most remarkable words said by an individual were Patrick Henry's, "Give me liberty or give me death."

Which reminds me of the sixth grade history buff who always finished every theme with that famous quotation, "Give me liberty or give me death." The teacher became so put out with the same quotation on every theme she decided to give an assignment whereby he would not be able to use it, so the title of the next theme was supposed to be "Horse Colic." The papers were all turned in, and she immediately thumbed through the papers to little Patrick Henry. And he wrote: "Horse Colic. Horse colic is something that is found in horses. It is found in the stomach of horses, and it is caused by gas pains hollering "Give me liberty or give me death."

But the words immediately before that famous challenge by the American patriot were perhaps equally courageous. He said, "But as for me"—which has to be among the greatest examples of an individual accepting his responsibility.

All during my life I have heard a story that further exemplifies this (probably the first time was around 1958 when Lewis Timberlake from Stamford, Texas, was national vice-president of the Jaycees and had already been a friend of mine for two or three years).

He relates that in the hills of some state or country or kingdom there was the story of the old man who was known as so wise that people throughout the years looked to him for wisdom and judgement. One young person who had left the community and acquired a college education told some of his buddies how he was going to test the old man. "I'm going to get a bird and hold it in both hands and let some of the feathers show and ask the old man if the bird is dead or alive. If he says it is dead, I will open my hands and let the bird fly away. If he says it is alive, I will crush the bird and drop it at his feet."

The young man went to the hills and confronted the old man just as he had told his friends, with the bird cupped between both hands and some of the feathers showing. When he asked the old man, "Is the bird dead or alive?" The old man looked down at the young man's hands very thoughtfully and said, "My son, that depends on you."

The key to the future depends on you. Before us stands the door to tomorrow. We have the key to that door. What belongs behind that door? Will we find our role in the world diminished as some have predicted? Or will the future be filled with the opportunities that will expand our goal far beyond what it has ever been in the past?

More than twenty years ago, in my inaugural address as the incoming president of Lions Clubs International, I used ten little words from the greatest speech I had ever heard—ten two-letter words—"If it is to be it is up to me."

Hopefully, we will not find ourselves in the situation of a jury in West Texas that was involved in a very complicated case. They listened to the evidence for several days and selected a foreman and then deliberated for hours upon hours. Finally, the jury filed back into the jury box and the judge asked the foreman of the jury to stand. He stood and the judge asked him, "Have you reached a verdict?" He said, "Yes, Your Honor, we have."

When the judge asked for the verdict, the foreman took out a piece of paper, unfolded it, and said, "We the jury have decided not to get involved."

Along that line is the story of the city slicker who drove up to the country store. He noticed a group of men engaged in a game of checkers sitting on one side of the store's porch. On the other side of the porch was a fellow sitting in a rocking chair.

The city slicker, who was at the store to make a big sale and turn over a nice profit, decided he would go over and speak to the man in the chair. The man, who was enjoying a good chew of tobacco, had an old hound dog lying on the floor beside him. The city slicker, knowing something of the love that country people have for their dogs, decided that the way to impress the man in the chair was to be nice to the man's dog. So he walked over to where the man was sitting.

"Howdy, mister," the city slicker said. "Does your dog bite?" he asked. "Nope," replied the man, giving a good strong spit of his chewing tobacco. The city slicker reached down to pat the dog on the head. The dog responded by biting the man's hand. Finally, when the other man had managed to get the dog off the city slicker, he spoke to the man in the chair again.

"I thought you said your dog doesn't bite," the city slicker said. The country fellow, still sitting in his chair, gave another healthy tobacco spit and then spoke. "My dog don't bite. That ain't my dog."

One of the tragedies of our age is our unwillingness to be helpful when we can. We see people who are headed for trouble, people to whom we could be helpful, and we simply make no effort to assist them. The Italian poet Dante once had this to say about such people: "He who sees a need and waits to be asked for help is as unkind as if he had refused it."

Our generation is seemingly being influenced heavily by this policy of non-involvement. We see places where we could help, where our help is needed, and we turn away with the thought that it is none of my business. And that thought, that attitude, is totally false. If you can be of help to your fellow man, and he needs your help, then it is some of your business. We are all part of the family of man, and that makes us brothers.

Our reason for being in the world is to make a difference, to make it matter that we are here. And the finest way we can do that is to lend assistance where and when we can.

To have an opportunity to do good—and to fail to take advantage of that opportunity—is a reflection of a tragic flaw in our moral character. Non-involvement is a self-defeating attitude because the time will come, for each of us, when we ourselves will need the assistance of another.

The apostle Paul wrote: "Be kind to each other." That is still good advice today. And the carpenter Himself said: "Treat others as you would want them to treat you." From experience let me say that advice takes precedent over a policy of non-involvement any day of the week.

In other words, if it isn't your dog, tell the man so!

But how can we as individuals on one hand continue to improve our own self image and successes and at the same time be a part of a larger involvement?

Here's a great exercise to show the relation between the one and the many, the great and the small.

Select a large box and place in it as many cannon balls as it will hold. There will be some spaces between the cannon balls; add large marbles until the box will hold no more. But you will find you can shake the box until more marbles can be placed in it. Then you might think it would be full beyond all question—but there would be room for some smaller type buck shot between the larger elements. Then you could pour in some finely granulated sand—and there would still be room to add some water. And after it all settled, there would still be room for more buckshot, sand, or water.

Now, relate that demonstration to your project, your community, or any group. Where there is no space for the great, there may be room for the little. When the little cannot enter, the less can make its way, and where the less is completely shut out the least of all may find ample room to enter.

You have to fill all the spaces to do a job well, and whether you are a cannon ball or a marble or a grain of sand—or the drop of water that fills the smallest space—there is a place for you, and there is a time for you, whether it be a year or a moment to relieve somebody for a bit.

You have the choice in your decision. In our global world this was emphasized to me when I was traveling in Lions Clubs International and was visiting a project on the Island of Cyprus, one place that I had no idea that I would ever have the opportunity to visit.

We were visiting a cornea transplant center, and they were naturally very proud of their project, and as they escorted me from room to room, they kept telling me this was an international project. I finally asked, "What do you mean, because we are all a part of the international organization?" The doctor explained that in the country of Cyprus they are not able to obtain the corneas from individuals because of government restrictions, so the corneas are furnished by the Lions of Sri Lanka, who put the corneas on Singapore Airlines furnished by the Lions of Singapore and transport them to Cyprus, where the operation is performed by Japanese instruments furnished by Japanese Lions in a building which was furnished by American Lions, and the first $30,000 was provided by the Lions Clubs International Foundation.

That is an example of a globally-combined, individual effort of many individuals and groups doing their jobs and filling all the spaces to accomplish great things no individual or group could accomplish alone.

Yes, we live in a global world, and what better example could there be of individuals than the four corners of the earth individually involving themselves with others to provide one of the senses, the opportunity to see. But perhaps more important is to know that there were many individuals who cherished the values of caring and sharing.

As a practical matter, there are only as many minutes in the hour as you use.

Everyone in the world starts with one thing: the same amount of time. The question is what we do with our time. I believe it was Dennis Waitley who described time as being an equal opportunity employer. Rich people can't buy more time, as time is very definitely an equalizer among rich people, paupers, and everyone between. Scientists can't invent new minutes, and you can't save time to spend it on another day. Many years ago I read something about the hour glass and bought one that still sits on my desk. It is not used to time my long distance calls or to time the boiling of an egg in my office—not even as a timing device for billing purposes. It's my reminder of the value of time.

If you turn an hourglass over and watch the thousands of tiny grains of sand tumbling down, you will notice that there is a great deal of activity going on there. Every one of these little grains of sand is on the move. But watch closely and you'll see that only one grain of sand at a time can move through the tiny neck of the glass. I, too, have many things to do, but this gadget helps me to concentrate on one job until it is properly done. It sometimes comes back to haunt me. All my legal assistants and secretaries have known about my hourglass reminder, and I have come into the office on occasion to find that somebody had turned the hourglass over to remind me to get back to the program of the day.

It's a waste of—well, time—to look for more time in a day. But we can use time more wisely. For most of us, one of the more popular excuses is, "I don't have the time"; but in the majority of cases this is just one of the many excuses along with "the fall season is starting," "someone else can do it," and "If I don't think about it maybe it won't be a problem."

There is a time to let things happen and a time to make things happen.

The first step in any type of time trap is, of course, to recognize the dilemma and then to prioritize our daily course of action. We cannot continue to live at the speed of light and disregard communication and relationships with others. We all start each day with the same opportunity—a time deposit is placed in our life bank each and every day of 1,440 minutes. Secondly, to everything there is a season and a time to every purpose under heaven (Ecclesiastes 3:1), which along with the other seven or eight verses graphically portrays the different season of time for each of us regardless of our time or station of life.

Today is an important day, and no matter how we spend it we traded a day of our life for it. It is a gift, but it is up to each of us how we use it. We can squander it, invest it, give it, or lose it, but we can never hoard it. Will we use it wisely?

Chapter 9

Values Give It All Meaning

Have you ever read the story by O'Henry about the prankster who invaded a merchant's showcase one night? He proceeded to rearrange the price tags on the items in the display window. The more expensive items were given the tags from the cheaper articles and vice-versa. Imagine all the possibilities for confusion and embarrassment when business opened the next day. There was chaos.

Some of it has been the work of pranksters, and some we've brought on ourselves, but there has been chaos concerning everybody's values during the last forty years. The 1960s were known as the decade of protest, the 1970s the decade of narcissism, the 1980s the decade of attitudes. The 1990s were expected to be the years of values—and I think many of us became more conscious of values. But as we get into the twenty-first century, I firmly believe and hope we are going to see such values more in evidence.

Then what are our values? Let's talk basics.

One of the greatest football coaches of all time, Vince Lombardi, was a fanatic about fundamentals. The people who played under him often spoke of his intensity and his endless enthusiasm for the guts of the game. Time and time again he

76

would come back to the basic technique of blocking and tackling. On one occasion the Green Bay Packers lost to an inferior squad, and it was bad enough to lose, but to lose to that team was absolutely inexcusable.

He called a practice the next morning. The men sat silently, looking more like whipped puppies than a team of champions. They had no idea what to expect from the man they feared the most. Lombardi walked into the room gritting his teeth and staring holes through one athlete after another. Finally, he said, "Okay, we go back to the basics this morning."

Holding a football high enough for all to see, he continued to yell, "Gentlemen this is a football."

How basic can you get? He's got guys sitting there who have been playing on gridirons for fifteen to twenty years who know offensive and defensive plays better than they know their kids' names, and he introduces them to a football. That's like saying, "Maestro, this is a baton." Or "Librarian, this is a book." "Mother, this is a skillet." "Marine, this is a rifle."

But the simplest philosophy worked. Lombardi believed that excellence and greatness could be best achieved by perfecting the basics of the sport. And he did well enough that the Super Bowl trophy is named after him decades later.

Know your position in life. Know your position. Learn how to do it right. Then do it with all your might.

Are basic values difficult to ascertain?

One of the most remarkable experiences I ever had was on a visit to the Hadley School for the Blind in Chicago, Illinois. Prior to the formal meeting I had an opportunity to meet Geraldine Lawhorn. She had been a personal friend of Helen Keller and also had what I thought was the same handicaps of not being able to see or to hear.

During the introductions as I was sitting next to Ms. Lawhorn, I noticed there was another person sitting on her other side. She was holding the director's hand in her own and using her fingers to tap in Ms. Lawhorn's hand. I finally realized the aide was translating the words that were being said to Geraldine Lawhorn by tapping in the palm of her hand. It was the only form of communication Geraldine Lawhorn had at that very moment with the outside world. The thought raced through my mind. Oh, what a tremendous handicap she had.

But then Ms. Lawhorn stood up to speak, and I will never forget what she said.

"It is better to know than to see; it is better to understand than to hear."

She was not the one with the handicap; I was the one with the handicap.

Why did she have such a zest for life? Because there were two values—knowing and understanding—that were more important than the two senses—seeing and hearing—she had lost.

When should we try to determine basic values?

Danny Cox, the ex-fighter pilot who tried to take off in the jet that would eventually reach a speed of 1,200 miles per hour often told his navigator that during the flight if he said "eject" the navigator better not say "huh?" because he would be talking to himself.

That is exactly where we are today—we've been talking to ourselves. It is time for action. Weak is he who lets his thought control his actions and strong is he who forces his actions to control his thoughts.

Yes, it takes time for us to find the answers to the basics of values even though we have been groping for thirty years, but I think we have been saying "huh?" too many times.

But we have learned one thing: success does not come to you, you go to it. You don't buy it with green stamps; there is no paycheck until the work is done; you don't get a report card unless all of the homework is in. Success is a matter of mind, time, attitude, and patience.

Every part of the American scene needs a return to the basics. Whenever you see fragmentation and failure, there you notice a drift from the basics.

The schools have drifted from the basics, and that to the regret of society, the home, the child. The schools need a return to the basics if disciplines are to be taught, if direction is to be given, and if life is to be equipped for living and relationships.

The church needs a new appreciation for the basics, lest it drift from the truths that give it meaning and reason for existence.

Government needs a new appraisal of the basics of the political process. For only where the basics of government are incorporated and followed will there be a constituency accepting leadership rather than a constituency promoting anarchy.

Adversity and/or Courage

It was in October of 1982 after a week-long Lions International board meeting in Johannesburg, South Africa.

Prior to the board meeting in any location, the president always visits and inspects the facilities and the planned events. Past International Director Dennis Gravenstein, a patent lawyer, and his wife Madge were chairing the host committee. We could not have been more fortunate, as they—along with the South African Lions—had everything well planned, with a visit to the world famous Krueger Park and then a split of the board members to visit Durban, Port Elizabeth, and Capetown.

Some eighty or ninety people boarded three separate planes that would hold twenty-five to thirty people and were headed for Krueger Park.

Everyone was in very jovial spirits after having completed a good board meeting and looking forward to experiences of seeing animals in the wild. Everyone drew for tickets, and Jay and I happened to be on the second plane—despite the fact that I was international president at the time.

When we arrived at the airport, the first plane had already arrived in this remote area, and the people were heading for the camp where we were going to spend a couple of nights. We checked our bunk houses and then got into a truck and rode out into the park as we had a couple of hours of daylight and the opportunity of seeing at least a lion kill—which you are not able to do on any particular excursion.

After we returned, I was in the souvenir shop and started checking with some of the other people to determine if they had seen any of the occupants of the third plane. One of the guides had told me earlier that the third plane had to do a little circling and was on its way.

Suddenly, somebody called me out of the souvenir shop

and took me to the airport several miles away, and told me there had been a crash and they were in radio contact with the group. We knew nothing of the extent of injuries or fatalities, and you can imagine my consternation and grief. Our first word was that somebody had been able to walk and hail down someone who had gone for aid.

In the first place, I was horrified at word of the crash because not only were these people all friends and associates—some of them very close and long-time friends from home—but I couldn't help thinking somebody had known about the crash for some time, and I felt, as the man in charge, I should have been told immediately. But at the moment everything was secondary to word of the condition of the occupants of plane three—including the likes of a past president of Lions Clubs International and a lawyer friend of mine since I was a child.

With more radio contact, we finally determined there were probably no fatalities but most of the occupants were injured in some way and most of them in such a condition that they were going to have to be transported to the hospital in Johannesburg—and they were not going to be able to fly but were going to have to be transported by buggy.

I returned to camp with a heavy heart, but I didn't want to panic everybody before I had more details myself. So I told only Jay about the crash and said it was anticipated they would try to transport those that were injured the least to the park.

As soon as the first ones arrived and I found out something about the extent of the injuries and that there were no fatalities. Even Past International President Herb Petry and Jo suffered injuries in that plane accident. I called the group together and explained to them that the plane had lost radio contact and had crashed into a very grassy area—which was fortunate, particularly since the plane had landed just a few feet before it would have gone off the top of a mountain.

Then I called all the other officers together, and we worked for the next ten or twelve hours—through most of the night—manning what radio and telephones were available, making arrangements with the hospital and transportation of the more seriously injured into Johannesburg.

I don't believe I could have done it by myself or without

Past International Presidents Joe Wrobleski and Bert Mason, even though everybody rose to the occasion in the face of adversity. With individuals working together we accomplished what no one could have done. And it was also under somewhat adverse circumstances, because there had been a split in the top leadership of the board due to a difference in philosophy. But all that was laid aside, and there was a continuous spirit of cooperation and—as a result—achievement.

I even managed to get on a prearranged early flight the next morning and was in Johannesburg by the time the third-plane people arrived. Again I heard many stories about acts of heroism by Lions toward associates with whom they had not seen eye-to-eye on policy measures hours earlier. Even people with widely varying backgrounds and races, from Texas to New England and such different countries as India, Canada, and Ecuador had forgotten differences and taken time to comfort one another, hold hands, pass on inspirational thoughts, and generally perform in heroic patterns during a crisis.

Past International Director Bruce Murray from Canada was on that plane and served as a stabilizer and comforter to all those who were injured more than he. Bruce was selected from the second year directors to be a member of the executive committee, which included all the other officers. He served as the liaison between the officers and the board, and I could not have asked for anyone to serve in that capacity and to do the job that was expected of him better than Bruce Murray. He was efficient; he was loyal; much of the success of my program and the board's would have to be attributed to Bruce Murray.

He also became one of the guiding forces in the Canine Vision School in Canada near Toronto, and I had the pleasure of being present for the ground-breaking, the opening, and the fifth anniversary. In fact, I felt like I was part of it, but Bruce and the Canadian Lions were the driving force.

When I had time to think about it, I decided it was not only Lions but humanity at its best.

Another example of cooperation under fortunately less immediately questionable circumstances involved the perpetual crisis element of West Texas: simple water.

We like to think around Ballinger that only a few of the

most hardy of God's creatures have the faith and patience to depend on the elements of weather for rain to quench our thirst and moisture for crops—not to mention the joys of seeing the beauty of West Texas vegetation.

As we observe the first leaves of the mesquite (our most reliable harbinger of spring) and see the first grass roots spring upward, we realize our faith and patience have again been rewarded. For this reason, grass roots has been a term of deep endearment for my home area.

The significance dawned on me while listening to my good friend General Robbie Risner describe his some seven years as a POW in Vietnam, fifty-four months of his confinement in isolation—including ten months in total darkness. You can imagine that he was under intense physical and mental stress.

On one morning at daylight, after a particularly frustrating day, Robbie got down on the floor of his seven-foot-by-seven-foot cell and crawled under the bunk where there was a vent in the floor that allowed in fresh air from the outside. He saw a faint glimmer of light reflected on the inside of the vent.

Being curious, he put his eye next to the cement wall and discovered a minute crack in the construction that allowed him to see outside.

The hole was so small that all he could see was a single blade of grass.

One ray of light, one single blade of grass, but it represented life, growth, freedom, and the realization that God had not forgotten him.

From my appointment to the Upper Colorado River Authority in 1960, the term Stacy Lake was a dream and a hope for West Texans for drinking and crop water and grass roots for then and future generations.

Time after time I had watched the flood waters of Elm Creek and the Colorado River flow through Ballinger on the way to their final destination—the Gulf of Mexico. What a waste it appeared. My dream—together with most West Texans—continued until finally through the leadership of the Colorado River Municipal Water District and the tenacity of Owen Ivie and many individuals too numerous to mention, the dream became a reality.

The icing on the cake was the early filling of the reservoir to its capacity of more than 550,000 acre feet in less than two years—drinking water for the cities and towns of the large expanse of West Texas, a beautiful body of water and recreation ample for thousands. Stacy Lake was eventually named Lake Ivie for the man who was most responsible for its development, and it is still the epitome of grass roots people having the tenacity to overcome unfounded objections from the south, special interest groups and, yes, even the Concho Water Snake, to make a dream come true.

Now we must use and further develop this area. Just as we must "Think globally and act locally" in a global world, we must also "Think regionally and act locally" in West Texas. What is of benefit to one city or town in this area of West Texas is of benefit to the entire area.

Instead of trying to add years to life in this chaotic pursuit of the material things, we need to add life to years by enjoying the beauty of God's creative work, all of the quality people, grass roots living, and the protection of and use of the environment for quality living and especially Ivie Lake, twenty-five miles southeast of Ballinger, Texas.

Be proud of your grass roots—of which you probably think as much as we do of Ballinger.

Communication

It should go without saying that you can't get anything done—or keep anything from being done, if that's your goal—without letting others know what you want. And that gets down to one of the most important skills of leadership, service, and daily life and business: communication.

Let's again look at Geraldine Lawhorn, the mute, sightless administrator I mentioned earlier. As her aide was using her fingers to tap messages into Ms. Lawhorn's hand, that was the only form of communication the director had with the outside world; but she used it to get more done than most of us with full sight and sound.

For over nineteen centuries it has been proven that the

most effective means of communication is mouth to mouth—or whatever means one uses—as long as it is on a one-to-one basis.

When Coca-Cola first began to market its product in China, it did so using a phonetic version of the brand name, Koo-kah-koo-lah. Sales were not good, and nobody could figure why until someone pointed out that, when translated, Koo-kah-koo-lah meant, "Bite the wax tadpole."

Sales rose dramatically, however, after Coca-Cola made a slight change to Kah-koo-kah-lah, which means "May the happy mouth rejoice."

For an American example, a salesman who had a large western territory was driving through an Indian reservation when he saw a general store at the side of the road. He decided to stop to stretch his legs and see whether he could get a cold soda.

While he was inside the store buying the soda, the store owner struck up a conversation with him. "Did you see the old Indian sitting outside on the porch?" he asked. "He's really a wonder. He has an amazing memory. On your way out, why don't you ask him a question about something in the past, and see if he can't answer it."

Curious, the salesman approached the Indian. "I understand you have an amazing memory," he said. "Tell me, what did you have for breakfast last March 15?"

"Eggs," the Indian said.

"Well, that was pretty silly," the salesman thought to himself. "How do I know whether that's true or not?" Feeling slightly foolish, he went back to his car and drove off.

Shortly thereafter, the salesman was transferred to a new territory, and it wasn't until five years later that he returned to the area on vacation. Driving on the same road, he recognized the general store where he had stopped long ago. To his surprise, the old Indian was still sitting on the porch. On a whim, he stopped his car and walked over to the Indian. Holding up his hand in greeting, he said, "How!"

"Scrambled," the Indian said.

However, we must stop and think and do it now. If we discovered that we had only five minutes to say all that we wanted to say, every telephone booth would be occupied by people calling other people to stammer that they loved them.

"Attitude does make a difference."

Leaders are not born, they are developed, inspired, and inspire others.

Courageous author, medical missionary, explorer, and discoverer of Victoria Falls, Dr. David Livingstone spent most of his adult life living in primitive conditions in Africa. Between 1857 and 1865, he led a team on an expedition into Eastern and Central Africa which laid the foundation for Nyasaland. Although tiresome, fatiguing, and dangerous, Dr. Livingstone's work was to him a labor of love.

While exploring in Africa, Dr. Livingstone received a letter from some well meaning friends saying, "We would like to send other men to you. Have you found a good road into your area yet?"

Dr. Livingstone sent this message in reply: "If you have men who will only come if they know there is a good road, I don't want them. I want strong and courageous men who will come if there is no road at all."

One of my favorite stories, because it relates to a small town but yet relates a point, comes from Lewis Timberlake, a man I highly respect.

Lewis told about the time several years ago the screaming of a fire engine siren startled the residents of a small West Texas community out of their peaceful sleep. The volunteer fire department raced to the outskirts of town where they found the local Baptist church engulfed in flames. People came from all over town either to help fight the fire or to watch the burning church that most of them attended. They came dressed in robes thrown over pajamas and nightgowns and stood in their bedroom slippers to watch in sadness and awe as their church slowly disintegrated before their eyes.

The pastor of the church watched first the fire and then the faces in the crowd—most of whom were members of his congregation. As his eyes scanned the faces reflecting the brightness of the flames, he caught sight of a young man standing off to one side away from the crowd. The pastor hadn't seen this man before, so he walked over to introduce himself.

"I'm the pastor of the church," he said as he extended his hand in a friendly greeting. "I don't think I've ever seen you at church before."

"Preacher," he responded, "this church has never been on fire before."

Get excited. Be enthusiastic if you thoroughly believe that it can happen. That's what leadership is about. Maybe you can feel some excitement today, but it must not be just a one-day excitement.

Three little boys were waiting in the doctor's office for their shots. The doctor went to the first one, who was reading a *Popular Mechanics* magazine and said, "Johnny, what are you going to be when you grow up?" Immediately Johnny said, "I'm going to be a mechanic. I want to fix autos and make airplanes fly."

He then went up to Tommy, who was reading *Field and Stream*. "Tommy, what are you going to be?" Tommy, without hesitation, said, "I want to be a hunting and fishing guide. Yes, that's what I want to be."

The doctor went over to little red-headed, freckled-faced Billy, who was carefully examining *Playboy* magazine. When asked the same question, Billy thought for a moment and then said slowly, "I don't know what you call it, but I can hardly wait to get started."

Well, now is that time to get excited, to get enthusiastic.

To recognize the value of the leader you must recognize basic values and believe in them without qualification.

I read of a college professor who questioned the philosophy that only those people with positive attitudes are revered in life. After all, there's never been a monument built to a cynic—not that I know of anyway. So this professor, hoping to expose this philosophy as false, borrowed the college track team for a few days for an experiment. The professor divided the team into two equal groups—equal in number, in ability, in their physical stamina, and so on. When he finished, he was satisfied that the two teams were matched as completely as possible.

The professor then took the first team to the track and told them that they would be given a series of scientific tests as part of a study being conducted by the school. The purpose of the tests, he told them, would be to measure physical strength and endurance, agility, and physical stamina.

He went on to tell the men that he wasn't sure that they

could complete the tests because they were extremely difficult. But, he told them, they must try to do the very best they could. The team members started on the tests and tried to do their best, but 57% couldn't complete them.

The professor took the second team to the track. Again he told them the same thing he told the first team—that the tests were extremely difficult and he didn't think they could master them. But this time he added something new. He told the men that one of the labs at the school had developed a new pill that had a tremendous capacity to increase a person's endurance, strength, stamina, agility, and ability to perform. This time he said the purpose of the tests was to prove the power of this amazing new pill.

The team members willingly took what they didn't know to be salt tablets and proceeded to take the tests. Eighty-eight percent not only completed the tests, but, in some cases, broke records that they had previously held. When the professor wrote up the results of his study of the track team, he said, "I must learn one of two things from this test. Either there are some unusual properties in salt that I never knew about before or there is truth to the idea that what your mind can believe you can achieve. People can change their destinies by changing their attitude."

No matter what your situation, you must believe it will get better. Until you believe that, you won't be able to develop an attitude that expects to succeed, an attitude that expects the best in life—even if the best has to rise out of the ashes of the worst. What you believe does make a difference.

Chapter 10

Healthy Body and Mind are Foundational

I was reaching the final stages of producing this book.

I had a generous offer from a publisher—a top-line Texas publisher who understands what it is to be a Texan with something to say. In fact, the publisher was a fellow Baylor grad likely to understand me and my background even better. And since the contract had been signed as of this writing, I can now say it is the great Eakin Press of Austin. (I'm sorry to say its founder, Ed Eakin, died while production of this book was underway.)

He was also a publisher with the expertise, the scope, and the commitment to help me get the word out even beyond Texas (though I have known people who used to think you drop off the face of the earth when you leave the Lone Star State). And scope is important, not only because I have traveled countless thousands of miles, mostly in the service of Lions International in over fifty countries in one year, gathering the experiences and insights that are the core of this book, but because, in effect, this book and my dual career in law and the Lions has been very much a collaboration among myself and many, many others. So I wanted to share my thoughts with as many of those contacts as possible—not to mention readers everywhere who might benefit from my thoughts.

I took an armload of manuscript pages, revisions, notes, and my tape recorder to the mountains for an overall review.

Much of the original dictation and organizing was done in Colorado. At the time of this dictation, I am two or three miles up from the cabin, so I imagined I am 8500 to 9000 feet along the most beautiful river, Vallecito, and saw the beautiful formations of rocks, all of which eventually go north to the Continental Divide. It seems that in this near solitude I can finally think back and bring the experiences and philosophies of life into enjoyable and readable form. If I should ever produce another book in some form or fashion, I will be sure to bring my notes and speeches to Colorado, and again organize the material into readable form.

And it's hard for a professional Texan to admit it, but Colorado is a wonderful rest and recreation area for us, particularly our place near the Continental Divide that was built in 1962 by the Judge and Mimi (the grandkids' name for my mother).

It's a real cabin—not a fancy retreat in which you might as well be at home watching a Colorado travel documentary. There are two bedrooms and some extra beds for visitors. But it has a big picture window overlooking the river, and it's the ultimate place for getting away from it all.

For years in the nineties, I fished as I had in the seventies at Vallecito Lake for the kokanee—a fish derived from the salmon that only lives three years but has a rich, delicious meat.

I've tried to arrange schedules so we could spend more time in Colorado during the summer, and the fax and telephone help us stay in touch between Lions conventions and meetings of district governors, past district governors, camp directors, and leaders of Texas Lionism.

Our place happens to be in the most beautiful valley of Colorado. The river in front of the cabin roars all day and all night, and with the windows open that restful and eternal symphony of cold water over prehistoric rock is a soothing background to study, thoughts, and dreams—a constant reminder of God's gift of trees, water, and beauty.

For ten or twelve years during the height of our travels, Jay and I didn't make it to Colorado, and it was always a some day soon promise for us.

One of our first and most memorable visits was in 1988, after the Lions convention in Denver. Joining us were two of our favorite friends, Martha and Sten Akestam, past president of Lions International and certainly one of the outstanding presidents with his involvement in the Quest Program of youth against drugs and for learning skills; and another eventual past president of Lions International, "Pino" Guiseppe Grimaldi, and his wife Adriana also joined us. Pino was on the board of directors with me in 1972 and 1974 and was president in the late nineties—which may be a record for the trail to the presidency.

That was a whirlwind tour, as we went to Mesa Verde and Silverton and did all the tourist things in one day. Judge and Mimi visited friends while we entertained the Akestams and the Grimaldis that year.

One reason the cabin was ideal for studying this manuscript is the three-mile hike to the bridge from the end of the road and the three-mile return hike. So I always had time for head-scratching and ruminating between the cabin and the car. All of which is background for my late analysis of this material.

And among other decisions was the idea that I needed to emphasize the importance of three foundation elements for effectual leadership and service: health, family, and a supportive community. Hence, this chapter and the next.

Of course, the mind, with its billions of neurons, is part of the key to a healthy body and healthy soul too, and it must be trained and disciplined for whatever goals one seeks. We have many great inventions, including computers and e-mails and faxes and ebays and all those things with which I'm not too familiar and leave up to my able staff. But my observation is that there is no invention or discovery that will take the place of the human mind.

I guess my first awareness of health was after I became International Director in 1972. I realized I was about twenty pounds overweight and sluggish—which affected mind and soul.

I started jogging. If you can imagine, jogging was not popular in other countries, and as I jogged in Australia and elsewhere down through the years, such as Portugal, South America,

Japan—and even big cities of America—people would absolutely stare me down, wondering if I was crazy or showing off. But, aside from health, it was useful to jog early in the morning and get an idea of the layout and note areas to explore more fully.

In 1973 I started jogging on highways quite a bit, but somebody suggested I ought to be using a softer surface. So I started jogging on the school track in Ballinger. The only other jogger I knew at the time was School Superintendent Dick Richey, and we often jogged together.

Among fellow joggers were Grant Lee—who later reversed the trend and moved back to old Maverick in 2001, where his dad Levy owned land. Grant bought the interest of his brother Dr. Tipton Lee of San Angelo as they put in a pecan orchard on the land. Grant jogged with me some twenty years, sometimes with his beautiful and inspirational daughters Jana (now Dr. Pena, an emergency technician and teacher of other medical students at a Phoenix hospital) and Jennifer Ashti, who became a Dallas lawyer, and Julie Foreman, who worked in my office for a time, a graduate of ASU in San Angelo.

Another early jogger was Carolyn Allen, wife of head coach Randy Allen, who had a successful coaching career at Ballinger and later at Brownwood, and later at Abilene Cooper High School. He is now in his third year of coaching at Highland Park High School in Dallas where he has had two 10-0 seasons and is 6-0 for the season as of this writing and has won every regular season game. In 2001, as of this revision, he has won his first playoff game. Randy and his wife Carolyn are leaders in each of the Baptist churches in the towns and cities in which they have lived. Carolyn and Randy have to be two of the finest individuals and Christians, without being showy, and exemplary to all, and Jay and I have been close to them ever since their time in Ballinger.

I was running and jogging about a fifteen-minute mile in 1973 and started setting goals for a nine-minute mile. Then my goal was two miles around the track, which then clocked thirty minutes. There were several telephone poles around the track and I would add a pole a day or a couple a week from the original mile as I climbed the track ladder to two miles. Then I was jogging and my goal was sixteen minutes for two miles, I was jogging three miles in about forty minutes, and my goal for three miles was twenty-seven minutes. That was about all the time I could take, but occasionally I'd go four miles. I ran five miles in the White Rock Marathon one time, but only as a Lions representative.

I kept up the three-mile regimen until 1994, when I came down with shingles in my ear and settled thereafter on a half-walk, half-jog for about forty-five minutes.

I did lose weight, and certainly felt better. But in the late seventies—about the time I was starting to run for third vice-president of the Lions—I was diagnosed with hypertension and high blood pressure. I continued exercise and did reasonably well until 1984. My blood pressure had not descended, but I was still a member of the Lions board and always thought my blood pressure was a result of stressful activities.

I read about Cooper Clinic in Dallas and thought it would be helpful in preventive medicine. Dr. Cooper's list was full, but I was lucky to get Dr. Boyd Lyles, a young internist specializing in preventive medicine. He was excellent, and we hit it off even though he was from Oklahoma.

He started me on treadmill tests, and everything seemed to be satisfactory for the time being.

But on July 4, 1986, Jay and I were at a reception for the Lions board in New Orleans, getting ready to go out on a boat for the fireworks. First, I felt overly warm, so I went out in the hall and didn't feel any better, and I was a little nauseated. I talked Jay into going on the boat trip and said I was going back to bed.

But that didn't help, even when I took some cold and headache pills. I couldn't sleep.

I was about to call the hotel doctor when I recalled that Dr. Wellington Pearce of Ballinger was in New Orleans.

"Bull," as we called him in Ballinger, was a great football player who went to Rice University. Later in the mid fifties he was on the cover of *Life* magazine while he was at Cornell University assisting in one of the first heart surgeries. He had two brothers in Ballinger—also doctors—and I had visited with him the week before while sitting on a bale of hay at a Ballinger anniversary.

But getting a doctor in New Orleans on the Fourth of July?

He was at home, having a backyard barbecue, and he told me to go to Toro Hospital and he'd have everything set up.

I left a note for Jay and called a cab.

At the hospital, they immediately gave me nitroglycerine and put me out.

Jay was worried when she got to the hotel and found my note, but she called Norm Dahl, a good friend from Illinois since 1964, who had been on my board. He got a cab and brought Jay to the hospital. Many times later, she was transported to the hospital by the son-in-law of Mary Louise and now Past International Director Dan Cole.

Dr. Pearce ordered tests (and, again, I had one of my countless international experiences, as I was being served by a doctor from India and one from Mexico, along with Dr. Pearce) and a catheterization.

I spent a week in the hospital, but tests determined there was no need for any type of invasive procedure. It appeared there had been a mild heart attack with minor damage to a small descending artery.

After tests back at Cooper Clinic in Dallas, Dr. Boyd Lyles said if he were just giving me a check-up for insurance he wouldn't have said I had a heart attack.

But it rang my bell.

I continued my exercises and tried to be more conscious of my cholesterol through the admonishment of my local general practitioner Dr. William Pollan of Ballinger.

I had two angioplasties in 1990 and 1991, but they were not considered successful at the time and were performed on minor arteries.

I was antsy about signing a form approving heart by-pass surgery if necessary, and Dr. Schwade said he understood and swore he would use his best judgement—more confirmation that I had met one of the finest human beings in the medical field, firm but compassionate, intelligent in his field, and up-to-date with seminars in his field. Later, in our correspondnce, he was quick and candid in replies, and I thought, "Here's an example of service—within and without his profession—as he tried to care for others the way he would like to be cared for.

I have tried to follow the same attitude in my law practice—particularly since the earliest days, when there was surely some selfishness rather than selflessness.

Dr. Lyles was much the same as Dr. Schwade, although he had more of an everyday and preventive practice that included all those tests and modern techniques.

Dr. Schwade had a great bedside manner—and he had the same patient and informative style with Jay and Michelle that made us all feel more at ease.

The blockage in 1991 and 1992 in the main artery turned out to be 75% to 80%—which is close to needing an invasive procedure. But Dr. Pollan had been studying reversal of plaque; Dr. Dean Ornish in California agreed that it was possible.

Dr. Lyles and Dr. Schwade thought it might work if I believed in it. I said, "If anybody can do it, I can." I was that confident in my health goals and abilities.

I kept studying, but I continued my exercise program—although some people asked why I kept exercising if it wasn't doing any good.

I concentrated on reducing my cholesterol and limiting fat content in my food—not so much for weight control but for reduction of plaque. At one time I had my weight down to 165 pounds, but I thought it made me look thin and it didn't seem that useful in the plaque control.

This may help explain a common psychological situation for others: my blood pressure seemed to rise during any visit to the doctor's office. Dr. Schwade called it "white coat syndrome." And I have confirmed, with blood pressure tests taken at home or elsewhere, that the doctor's office does seem to raise my pressure. That's probably true for many others.

With some medicine for blood pressure and cholesterol, my health has been consistent—thanks to the Lord and my doctors.

In 1994 I had Bells Palsy and shingles inside my ear. I had never experienced such discomfort and pains. They were giving me medicine that was a grade down from morphine, and I had a reaction that lasted through the summer of 1995. I had constant ringing in the ears that sounded like a flock of birds, and it was very annoying.

A San Angelo doctor, Dr. Brian Humphries, suggested an extract from an ancient Chinese tree (ginkgo biloba)—and it worked and has kept working for more than five years as of this writng.

I've always believed in vitamins, and I've taken various vitamins recommended by the Cooper Clinic. I later switched to a Cooper multi-vitamin, which cuts down on the number of pills.

But I have been very healthy overall and have lost little time from work or Lions activities.

I was bothered with headaches in the eighties and was seeing Dr. David Pugh, an allergist of Abilene. He sent me to Dr. Atkins, an eye, ear, and nose specialist, and we still couldn't find the cause. Eventually, Dr. Pollan and Dr. Lyles became involved, and Dr. Lyles arranged for me to have several tests in Dallas with neurologists and other specialists, which included a nerve test and an electroencephalogram. But, again, to no avail.

Dr. Lyles finally sent me to a headache clinic in Houston, Texas, headed by Dr. Matthew Ninan, a superb expert in the field. It was a residency program of several days in which they take you off all medication and start over, checking each medication and reaction as they re-establish a regimen. And, after some discomfort and confusion, we came up with something that has given me optimum control.

They even found a medicine for the restless leg syndrome that had troubled me for years. My advice is: keep trying and don't delay going to a doctor.

That is surely more than anybody cares to know about the specifics of my health. But I went into some detail because your health is the next most important element after God and family—and even more important to your family than to you. It is not macho—it's just not good sense—to ignore symptoms of health problems. And, in line with our leadership and service theme, it should be obvious that a person can't lead who is in pain and can't be of as much service to others without being in control of his or her own body and mind.

It's all a part of my faith in the miracle of this life—that you can make of it what you will and you can make a difference for others.

I feel most fortunate that I have lived through all the medical and other problems and have managed to remain committed to helping others.

Chapter 11

Roots Do Count

In writing this book, I have tried to be careful not to suggest that I achieved some success as an attorney and public official and throughout the scope of Lions International because of some great ability of my own.

In the first place, it just isn't true; if it hadn't been for the firm, wise direction of Judge Grindstaff and the loving insight of Mother, to start with, I doubt that I would have acquired the ambition—let alone the skills—to do well in public life. And one of the great reminders of these recollections for me was the literally countless Lions of every type and color and station who gave their support from Ballinger to the worldwide panels of Lionism.

But, aside from avoiding the braggadocio element, cooperation and mutual support are crucial in every walk of life, and any concept of leadership without having a genuine respect for the foot soldiers, the fellow travelers, grass-root workers, amounts to some kind of despotism or exploitation.

While I have cracked jokes about being from a small town, I must emphasize here that—other than my parents—the luckiest break I ever got was growing up in Ballinger, Texas.

I'm often introduced as the guy who came from a little town in West Texas to become the top Lion in the world, and—while

I know it is meant as a compliment—I think it tends to give the erroneous impression that my small-town roots were something to overcome.

In fact, I think small-town values are a blessing, a solid foundation, and a bulwark against big-town influences that may confuse and mislead.

The longer I live, the more I realize the things that really count in life—integrity, drive, respect for others and for my God and theirs, and a firm sense of the way things work in society— I learned in Ballinger.

Of course, I think Ballinger is special. You probably think the same of your hometown, and that's what makes the world go round.

I must note that some of my Lion heroes came from small towns—people like Herb Petry from Carrizo Springs, a town of about 7500; Tex Mayer from La Grange, a town of about 5500.

But I'll never forget the all-out effort of my fellow Ballingerites in support of my Lions career. Such was the case at the convention in Montreal in 1979, where my drive for the presidency actually got under way.

We had started more than two years in advance, lining up the likes of the "World Famous Cowboy Band" of Hardin-Simmons University in Abilene for the Montreal parade. Now, the Lions convention parade is usually about as big and exciting as the Rose Bowl or Macy parades, in part because of the world-wide diversity of the elements, costumes, and marching units.

But as they say in Abilene, "You ain't seen nothin' till you've seen the Cowboy Band," with its cowboy regalia in the fast-paced "cow kick," its pretty girls on six big white horses, and its ropers (one of whom caused a stir by roping a president during a Washington, D. C. parade). And it was particularly appropriate at Montreal because both the Judge and my mother were graduates of Hardin-Simmons.

Lions District Director Dr. Bill King arranged for the Cowboy Band, but it was expensive and consumed most of the parade budget of the Lions of Texas. And we wanted to get the Ballinger band to Montreal. A great band in its own right, the Ballinger band had been known for outstanding performance both as a marching unit and in concert since the early 1940s. (I was a member of it for some five years, first chair clarinet, and voted outstanding senior band member—while doubling in football during the season.)

But we discovered it was going to cost about $30,000 in 1979 dollars for transportation, housing, food, and the like—after each band member had made a small contribution for the trip. But that was no barrier to Baylorite John King, whose son Joel was in the band, and who had been involved in everything from the Baptist Church to Rotary Club to Chamber of Commerce, City Council, and a big supporter of Ballinger Lions Club.

With the Ballinger Band Boosters, we pursued bake sales, chili suppers, hot dog suppers, fish fries, pancake breakfasts, pancake suppers, barbecued chicken, "pile-ons"—everything imaginable, including pledges from companies and individuals.

But that wasn't near enough money.

Then a large truck hauling apples from Washington State turned over near Ballinger. King was in insurance, and he arranged for the apples to be donated to the band's travel project.

For the next three months, apples were sold on the highways and byways and in the homes, and if it's true that apples are healthy, Ballingerites had to be the healthiest people anywhere that year.

But they put the Montreal fund over the top, and the Ballinger band was a mainstay of the Texas delegation at the convention.

The band was great for my campaign, great for the convention, and—as John Fiveash reminded me some fifteen years later at the grocery store—great for the kids. Many of these kids had never been past Abilene or San Angelo. Now they had seen another world—thanks to a lot of people who believed in the band, believed in the kids, and believed they could make a difference. And they did.

And the Ballinger Lions—for at least the sixty or so years I know about—have been as devoted as the community they have supported for more than seventy years. And I flatly could not have gotten out of town on my trip to International President without their help and support.

As of this writing, I received word of the death of Price

Middleton, who with his wife Ann had been friends of Jay's and mine forever. He was a prime example of what Lionism—and public service—are all about.

I was elected district governor in 1964, and Price became cabinet secretary. Retired from the military during World War II, he wore an extra-high shoe for a disabled leg and foot. But there was nothng disabled about his mind or his skills—both with records and with people. Price was quite a politician himself; he had helped both Judge and me in political races and was county auditor for years.

Other senior members of those Ballinger Noon Lions were Joe Ed Burnam, Dr. Oran Chandler, Dick Ayers, Cal Adair, Rocky Stone, R. D. Travis, Jr., Elliott Kemp, George Beard (who became the third district governor of the Ballinger Noon Lions Club), J. B. Arrott, Jerry Willingham (president 1983-'84), Joe Kozelsky, Odell Howard, Darrell Rains (president 1982–'83, while I was international president), Norval Meredith, Gene Davis, Leo Williams, Charles Shepard, Aubrey Faubion, Max Pratt, Doug Wadsworth, Doug Cox, Rodney Gordon, Fred Harwell, Jr. (who has probably been a director of the Ballinger Lions Club more than anyone in history and was president of the Lions Club both at Brownfield and Ballinger) and in later years, Joe Nation and Newman Smith (peerless historian of Ballinger and Runnels County), Robert Wilson, Jimmy Caughron, Mark Travis, Sam McLarty (of the Ballinger Breakfast Lions Clubs). All of these and many others played an important role in the life of their respected clubs and our international campaigns.

About 1995, the Ballinger Lions seemed to be getting a little long in the tooth—even though we had the finest people in the world—and we started recruiting. Jerry Willingham and I were able to enlist his son Mark, a member of the band at Montreal who had been in real estate in Austin but returned to Ballinger. By coincidence, we arranged for son Jerry to join the Austin Downtown Lions Club and he eventually became president and also zone chairman, and later son Todd became a member of a Houston Club.

Then Mark and I enlisted Joseph Toliver, and Mark and Joseph rounded up another half a dozen new Lions in their thirties. Dr. Mark Bacigalupi became president of both the local

Lions and the District Eye Bank—with which he has made several trips to Central America to train others for eyeglass recycling and other aspects of eye care.

Two long-time friends of mine, Weldon Brevard and Rudy Hoffman, transferred from the Breakfast Club. Rudy had worked for NASA Space center before becoming a stock farmer and a great citizen of Ballinger—from city administrator to city council and mayor. His wife Jo worked at the First National Bank of Ballinger, and was also greatly involved in community affairs; Weldon was on the city council. Weldon had successful tenures as a football coach at Ballinger, Boswell, and Colorado City before coming back as Ballinger high school principal and junior high principal, and then taught history for several years thereafter. Weldon, along with his wife, Diane, who is a Ballinger native and who was an effective and popular junior high teacher, both served as role models to young people because they cared and were willing to do whatever necessary to direct them on the road to success.

During later years, one of my best friends was Bob Carothers, a baseball ace for Abilene High School, who played pro baseball for several years and then returned to obtain his degree at Baylor University. He has been my banking client and—more importantly—my golfing buddy for more than fifteen years. Bob and Ginny lived across the street from us for several years.

Among Ballinger Lions who went with me to Chicago for my first convention as a Lion (although I had attended three as a youngster with Judge and one in Mexico City after my graduation from Baylor) were John Purifoy, Rocky Stone, and Cal Adair. We stayed at the Palmer House in downtown Chicago, and Cal took over the piano while the house band was on break; Cal was so spectacular the crowd called for him even after the band came back.

There were many non-Lions at Montreal because of the Ballinger Band, and some nine Ballinger Lions at Hawaii—in addition to my guests Mark and Rhonda Goetz (my number one executive secretary for twelve years as we had six secretaries and three partners) and Ken (my law partner other than Judge) and Mary Slimp, in addition to my son Jeff and daughter Michelle.

Mike and Annette Butler of Kerrville (Mike later became a district governor and then an international director) began hosting dinners that started in Kerrville for the international guests that visited the camp and also the many future district governors of Texas. The hospitality extended all the way to Montreal and beyond. Mike and Annette handled all the chores in the hospitality room along with Marshall and Wanda Cooper, who is a past district governor (and later became president of the Crippled Childrens Camp and also an international director of Lions Club International). Both were from the Panhandle of Texas and the Beaumont area. All four of these were warm and entertaining to all of our guests and were absolutely indispensable during the convention in 1982 and in Hawaii in 1983.

It's so difficult to mention and thank all the Lions who were so dedicated during one or both of the campaigns: the Lions from my own District 2-A1 for the beginning and execution of our plans that included Past District Governors Homer Hodge, Paul Palmer, Harlan Brancell, Ben High, Oscar Cook, John Hancock, Leonard Hanson, Duke Jimerson, Lou and Jo Carothers, and all of the dedicated Past District Governors of District 2-A1, their Cabinets, the Ballinger Lions, and all other Lions in District 2-A1 and throughout the State of Texas. Other Lions from all over the state include: Past District Governor Pancho Luna (who provided his famous chips from Dallas, Texas, both at Mexico City and throughout all the highways and byways to Montreal); Past District Governors George Thompson, Alton Griffin, Dexter Anderson, and Loren Maples from Graham, Jim McNeil from Crosbyton, Roy Lynn Kahlich from Wilson, and Joe Sutton from Yoakum; Past District Governor Gerald Devault (who got his first touch of real Lionism working in the Montreal campaign), Don Hamilton from Tyler, Don Robinson from Houston—some of the most stalwart and dedicated past district governors who all were so dedicated to the cause of Lionism.

There were two very talented individuals from Texas who had performed in Texas and also been the lead performers at previous international conventions. There was Past District Governor Marion Snider from Dallas, who can play the piano like no one I have ever heard and who began his career with the

Stamps Quartette and has performed for many different groups since that time (in fact, he and Gordon were featured performers at Michelle's wedding in December of 1983 right after we went out of office) and Lion Gordon Rea who was a vocalist all over the state at different Lions functions and also at the international conventions. They gave the enthusiasm needed in Texas and at some of the meetings prior to the election and the convention proper for us to be successful as every delegate enjoyed their entertainment. They were both real performers and, frankly, it helped me get a lot of votes. Many, many thanks go to Marion and Belle and Gordon and Lavonne.

During the time I was going through the chairs to PIP, Lionism in Texas reached its top membership of 45,000 in May of 1983, and a lot of that growth of zeal and enthusiasm was exemplified by two of the most dedicated of all: Freddie Wolters from Bryan (another one of those Aggies) and my close friend since Mexico City, Roy Davis from Weslaco, who is married to Marlene.

Then there was the most famous Bill Melton, who was the golden voice of every sports network but who was also the master of ceremonies at one of my banquets in Atlanta. He was a graduate of UT who announced their games for years—as well as the games for the Texas Rangers and SMU. He is not only one of the great announcers of the southwest but truly a gentleman and a dedicated Lion who has served as county treasurer of Dallas County for over twenty years and has been president, I believe, of both the state and national treasurers associations.

Our base moved to Lubbock, Texas, for the Montreal drive under the able direction of Art Cook, while John Cook of the Lubbock Lions and the Lubbock *Avalanche-Journal* and Don Buckalew were instrumental in preparing what we thought was a very effectual brochure—in five languages—along with all the other "Ebb Tide" materials.

Past International Director Don Buckalew from Conroe kept us straight on campaign finances, because we didn't want to go to outside sources other than what we could raise and the funds provided by the council of governors directed by Jimmy Pigman.

My "Ride the Ebb Tide" campaign, of course, proved successful, thanks to the likes of all these Lions and friends. I was just the execution man.

The creativity and support had always been great.

In 1972, part of the paraphernalia was the biggest Texas pecans (another Homer Hodge idea) I'd ever seen, with key rings and the message "Ride the Ebb Tide." Ace Reid showed up for a dinner that year and did a caricature of me and told some of his hilarious stories. Phil Lorfing of Lowake Inn fame put on a chili dinner at Kerrville's Inn of the Hills and went with us to Mexico City. We entertained many Lions from South Africa to New Zealand at Lowake, and they were always amazed by the Texas breakfast, with a large beer stein of orange juice and a plate full of steak, eggs, hashbrown potatoes, and all the trimmings.

The real father of the Texas Lions Camp was Jack Weich, an attorney and past district governor from Brownsville, Texas, who actually served a year or two after Judge Grindstaff. He and some other stalwart Lions put together the idea and were able to get support from the federal government for the camp, which opened in 1953.

Jack continued to be the leader for the camp—and attended more than 100 semi-annual board meetings—service for which he was recognized at a gala affair in Kerrville about 1999.

Jack and I had worked together through the late sixties, and he was my inspiration to become an officer of the camp and president in 1969 through 1971.

For half a century, Texas Lions have been instrumental in making this camp a reality without cost to the kids.

There is no question in my mind that Texas has produced some of the most outstanding international directors to serve in our association, and it is a matter of record that we have had more Texan past presidents than any other state or nation.

But good Lions come from everywhere. In the 1983 convention, I invited Lions of Australia to present their Mint program which I observed was quite successful. After that, Ed Flood, past international director from Amarillo, was asked to be the director of this particular program; and then the Lions International Foundation was formed with Past District Governor John Petry and others who have served in that capacity throughout these seventeen years. A goal of a million dollars for the Texas Lions Foundation was met in 2000.

Other great Texas Lions include: Mike Butler from Kerrville; Marshall Cooper from Beaumont; Past International Director Howard Leverett of Houston; Past International Director Ray Hughston from Brownsville, who journeyed from College Station, Texas, to San Diego, California, on a bicycle for the 1999 convention; past International Director Jimmy Ross, who is now running for second vice president of Lions Club International; Connie de la Garza, first Hispanic director from Texas (elected mayor of Harlingen at the same time as his international race); my great vice-presidents including Past President Joe Wrobleski and Norma Jean of Pennsylvania, Past President Bert Mason and Beryl from Donaghee, Northern Ireland. There is also: bylaws chairman Bill Woolard from Charlotte, North Carolina, and finance chairman Dan Banker from California (you know that I had great help and direction in Bill, Don and Kajit, all three who became president of our association, and there were at least three others that were vying to run for a third vice-president and all of them would have been good presidents).

Furthermore, there are Past District Governor Norm Dahl of Illinois; Past President Dick Bryan of Ohio and later Arizona; and Directors Joe Camarda of Massachusetts; Kajit Habananda of Bangladesh, Thailand; and Hal Long of Oklahoma.

I cannot fail to mention Lions International staffers like Roy Schaetzel of Chicago (in well-earned retirement in Florida); and Chicagoans Lion John Stewart, Kaoru Anderson (interpreter for Past President Kay Murakami of Kyoto, Japan), Laura Heine, Carol Clemens, June Stricat, and Donna Beckett.

Things didn't just happen—they happened because of that caliber of people who wanted to make a difference, whether they were staffers or volunteers.

And I must add that—regardless of viable goals and great support—nobody wins everything all the time.

Judge Grindstaff was a low-keyed but consummate politician, and he said, "politics is a matter of timing"—which I didn't fully grasp until 1977, when we had planned to run for third vice-president of Lions International. But it just didn't seem to be the right thing at the right time.

So we regrouped for a major campaign in 1979. And since endorsements are only in effect for two years, we had to get repeat endorsements from everybody, and some of my friends in Texas said, "We voted for you two or three times; how many times do we have to vote for you?"

But they were generous in going along—even though there was another candidate from Pennsylvania doing all he could to reach Montreal with full backing. He dropped out four months before the July convention, but we were prepared to run at that convention with the whole world runnning against us, with all the literature, paraphernalia, and plans for a successful race.

It proved to be the right thing at the right time.

Chapter 12

Share the Vision of Service

Inaugural Address of International President
by Everett J. "Ebb" Grindstaff
1982, Atlanta, Georgia

In the fable of a bug that spent his entire life in the most beautiful Persian rug in the world, all the bug ever saw during his lifetime were his problems. He couldn't see over the top of them, and he had to bite his way through the wool to find some crumbs that someone had spilled on the rug and then to move to another place where he might find some more crumbs. This is the way he spent his life. Rather a "crumby" life!

The tragedy of the bug in the rug was this, that he lived and died in a most beautifully designed rug, but he never knew that he spent his lifetime in something that had a pattern. Now if that bug had risen up, he would have been able to see that the rug had a pattern and that problems were a part of that pattern. He would have also seen that the pattern was beautifully designed and unique, offering the opportunity of a lifetime because of the uniqueness of the creation if the bug had had a different point of view.

My point of view is that I am not here on this earth by

chance. I am here for a purpose, and that purpose is to be of service to my fellow man. That purpose is to grow into a mountain—not shrink into a grain of sand. All problems, discouragements, or heartaches are in truth great opportunities in disguise. No beast, no plant, no wind, no rain, no rock, no rake had the same beginning as I, for I was conceived in love and brought forth with a purpose.

My point of view has been nurtured and blessed, because I have been fortunate in having my dad and mother who indelibly impressed service on my mind at a very young age. Because of the opportunity to attend my first International Convention in 1946 as a mere lad of fifteen, I was able to see men of character and strength stand tall and lead our association to greater heights even though the times were perilous. I also had the opportunity to observe the results of people giving unselfishly of their time and efforts in order to make this world a better place in which to live. However, if we are to continue to live together successfully, we must be able to share the vision of service.

There is no question that the decade of the eighties will be the most challenging in history. We live in a time and under conditions that have never before existed. In just a few hours we can go anywhere on this planet, and what happens in one part of the world will affect each of us regardless of where we might live: in the city or on the farm or in a small community; it will affect us regardless of our homeland. This is why we have the greatest challenge that has ever existed for Lions Clubs International, the world's largest and most active service organization. We have an opportunity to significantly influence human minds and human thinking, living, caring, sharing, and acting.

Yes, you and I, part of the more than 1.3 million Lion family have this influence. But we must be optimistic in our thinking, optimistic in our actions, and optimistic in our living.

You put some fleas in a jar, and they'll start jumping and hit the top. But the longer they jump, you'll soon notice if you watch carefully, that they're not able to hit the top, even though they're still jumping. You can even take the top off the jar, and they will never jump out, because they have conditioned themselves to only jump so far. And so it is with people and the world of negativism in which we live today. People sit and do not reach their goals because they have conditioned themselves to only do so much, to only get by. This is why I don't like Lions to be referred to as average. Why? You know what average is: average is what failures claim to be when their friends and families ask them why they are not more successful; average is the top of the bottom of the top.

Which of these are you? Average means run of the mill, mediocre, insignificant. Being average is a lazy person's cop-out. It's lacking the guts to take a stand in life. It's living by default. Being average is to take up space for no purpose, to take up the trip through life but never pay the fare, to return no interest for God's investment in you. Being average is to pass one's life away with time rather than to pass one's time away with life. The successful are remembered for their contributions, the failures are remembered because they tried. But the average are just forgotten. To be average is to commit the greatest crime one can against oneself, humanity, and one's God. The saddest epitaph is this: Here lies Mr. and Mrs. Average. Here lies the remains of what might have been except for their belief that they were only average.

Sooner or later a Lion, if he's wise, learns that life is a mixture of good and bad days, victory and defeat, give and take. He learns that it doesn't pay to be too sensitive a soul; that he shouldn't let some things go over his head like water on a duck's back. He learns that he who loses his temper usually loses out. He learns that the quickest way to become unpopular is to carry tales and gossip about others.

He learns that it doesn't matter so much who gets the credit just so long as the service is performed. He learns that even his worst enemy is human, and it doesn't hurt to say "good morning" even if it's raining. And he comes to realize that most of his fellow Lions are as dedicated as he is, and that they have brains just as good or better than his and that hard work, not cleverness, is a secret to successful service. However, just remember that new objectives can be reached. Look at how long it took for a person to break the barrier in running a mile in less than four minutes. It couldn't be done because people had conditioned themselves that it could not be done. But then, Roger Bannister did it, and only a few weeks later someone else did it, and since that time over 500 people have broken the four-minute barrier, including one person thirty-six years of age.

Unfortunately, many people make poor use of life. They seem almost to resent it. It irks them, it hurts them, disappoints them. Drink, drugs, lack of faith, wrong living, and wrong thinking leave human beings in ruin, pitiful wrecks of what God meant them to be. Many a young person with talent, people with ability, with a bright future, throw life away or hide their talents as did the man in the Bible. Self-distrust has ruined many a good life. Laziness is a terrible thing. Indecision, jealousy, and all forms of fear are saboteurs. God gave each of us some talent, some time. This is the only health we have. If we fail to develop our talents, we will likely waste forty years of life. If I waste my time and fail to develop my talents, I have stolen from my community and from God the services I might have rendered.

Success in life depends on the motive. If you are in the race merely for the fun of it or for a meal ticket, you will not put the same energy into your running as you will if your ambition is deeper and more serious.

Life is somewhat like a grindstone, it either polishes you or reduces you to dust. It depends on you.

What is it that people like to see the most? Well, let me give you one language that is all its own, a time-proven universal language understood by people of every nation. Indeed, we may not speak the same tongue as our neighbors, but there's one thing that we do that has no language barrier: we smile in the same tongue. There is no interpreter needed for this expression of love, happiness, or good will.

When you meet the man without a smile, give him one of yours. A smile costs nothing but gives much. It enriches those who receive, without making poorer those who give. It takes but a moment, but the memory of it sometimes lasts forever. It brings rest to the weary, cheer to the discouraged, sunshine to the sad, and it is nature's best antidote for trouble. Yet it cannot be bought, begged, borrowed, or stolen, for it is something that is of no value to anyone until it is given away. Some people are too tired to give you a smile. Give them one of yours, as no one needs a smile so much as he who has no more to give.

A smile is a curve that can set lots of things straight.

When you do not know what to do or which way to turn, smile. This will relax your mind and let the sunshine of happiness into your soul.

A smile is a mystery; nobody knows its biological cause, only its emotional effect. For the person who smiles feels better himself. His smile is not only light to another's spirit, its curve swings inevitably back to light his own.

A smile is the light in your window that tells people there's a caring, sharing individual inside.

However, there is one other attitude that will tear down all the smiles, all the good will, warm feelings, and fellowship that we might have built. Unfortunately, it also exists in the world's greatest service organization, an organization that must live and act unselfishly. Here we are, the world's largest service organization and we are supposed to perform in an unselfish manner. It is time that we lay aside selfish interest and personal prejudice about people. We must look at the total picture and common good for all. We do not need to criticize unless it is constructive. If you take pleasure in unconstructive criticism, it is time to hold your tongue. If you must slander someone, don't speak it, but write it in sand near the water's edge. Gossip, whether it's true or not, is like mud on the wall. You can wipe it off, but it leaves a spot.

Only when these elements are exercised can we fully unite and truly become the world's leading force. Wild geese fly seventy percent further and longer because they fly in formation. Each shares the load of leadership, and the wind tunnel they create makes it possible to go further. Any silly goose knows that if you try to go at it alone, you'll never make it.

Yes, the time to begin is now. The man who moves mountains begins by carrying away a small stone. We must give of ourselves because rings and jewels are not gifts. They're only apologies for gifts. The only true gift is a portion of yourself.

The need is there and that's why we are here. We must be aware of that need.

An executive for a very wealthy man was standing with his boss in a penthouse of a skyscraper in a large city. He was trying to illustrate his point of view to his boss, and called him over to the window and asked him what he saw below. The boss said he saw only a mass of people. The executive then took him into the next room and on the opposite wall was a very large mirror and the executive asked the boss what he saw. I see only myself, said the man.

The executive said that is his point. The glass in the window and the glass in the mirror are the same, but there has been a little bit of silver tinge added to one, which has changed the view. So it is with people. Because of their viewpoint, instead of seeing the mass of people with all their needs, we see only ourselves.

If we are going to serve the needs of the masses of people crying for help, we must not work against each other. We must work together.

Two donkeys stood in the middle of a pasture, both tied— a bucket of hay to the right, a bucket of hay to the left. The hard-headed donkeys continued to pull against each other and both were denied necessary food. Had they had the good sense to come together, they either would have been able to go to the left or the right and to share the food of life and be blessed and sustained. Of course, this does not mean to surrender basic vital principles, but it does mean that we can do so much more when we join hands together.

We all control our destiny. We are the masters of our emotions, and unless our mood is right they will generate failure. People do not depend upon the weather to flourish, we make our own weather. If we bring rain, gloom, darkness and pessimism to people around us, they will react the same. If we bring joy, enthusiasm, brightness, and laughter, others will react favorably.

In a certain part of the world, young bulls are tested for the fight arena. Each is brought into the ring and allowed to attack a picador who pricks them with a lance. The bravery of the bull is carefully determined according to the number of times he demonstrates his willingness to charge in spite of the sting of the blade.

This is the challenge or test that we also have.

If we persist, if we continue to try, if we continue to charge forward, we will succeed. The prizes in life are at the end of each journey and not at the beginning. We do not know how many steps are necessary in order to reach our goal. We may still encounter failure at the end of the one-thousandth step. Success may yet hide behind the next bend in the road. Let's take another step, and if that is another failure we will take another and yet another. In truth, one step at a time is not too difficult.

(Left) Aunt Ora, Mother, Judge, and Ebb on their way to Maverick

(Below) Early days

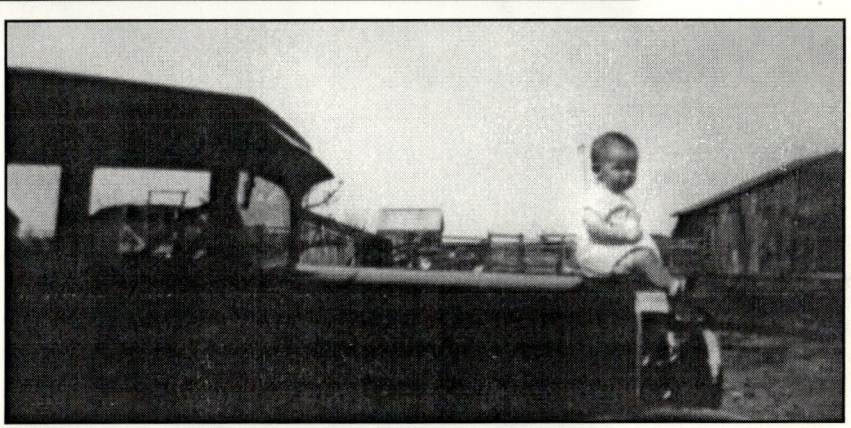

(Left) Ebb on his first ride

(Below) Family picture of Mother (when she was teaching at the Mexican school), Judge, and me, 1938

(Top left) Successful fishing trip at Mertzon with (l-r) Judge, Ebb, and Levy Lee during World War II

(Top right) High school football in 1944

(Bottom) The Rhythm Band—Ebb is the fourth from the left on the top row, Wart Hill, second from left, and Bob Agnew, tall one on the bottom left.

(Above) *Mineral Wells High School graduates, E.C. Grindstaff standing front row, right.*

(Left) *The four Grindstaff brothers: bottom left, Uncle Isaac, cotton buyer in Haskell, Texas; my granddaddy, James Everett Grindstaff; top left, Uncle Henry, lawyer in Haskell, Rotan, and Roby; and, Uncle Lige, lawyer in Weatherford*

(Below) *High school days*

Graduating class at Maverick; Judge was superintendent

(Left) My Uncle Henry, Uncle Lige, and my great-granddaddy Elijah Grindstaff in the corn field, cuffing top fodder above the ear and piling it around the stalk

(Below) Senator Lyndon B. Johnson politicking in front of Keel Drug Store in Ballinger with avid listeners; from left A.F. Brock, Judge, R.E. Bruce, Levy Lee, and Jack Moore

(Above, left) Ebb and Jay on their honeymoon at Horsetail Falls in Monterrey, Mexico

(Above, right) Senate majority leader Lyndon B. Johnson autographed: To my friend, E.C. Grindstaff, late 50s

Ebb with Ballinger Lions President Charles Shepard at Flag Project, 1969

(Top left) Following the local custom in Tunisia in 1979

(Top right) Ebb with Ballinger Lions President Norval Meredith at Ballinger's historic Carnegie Library, 1978

(Middle) The Ballinger High School Bearcat Band

(Bottom) Texas delegation marching, and Ebb and Tex Mayer (shaking hands with the audience) when elected as International Director in Mexico City in 1972

(Above left) The president and his wife, Jay; son, Jeff, and daughter, Michelle, holding Callie the family cat, relax at their Ballinger home, 1978

(Above right top) Ebb with Texas Lions campers

(Above right bottom) Ebb with campers at Texas Lions Crippled Children's Camp in Kerrville, including Gene Hash from Ballinger

Ebb with Texas Lions campers

Clockwise from top left:
Roy Davis and Ed Flood campaigning
Ebb trying to get in shape for the run as presi-
dent
Jay and Ebb playing tennis in Ballinger
Early send-off with caricature by Ace Reid

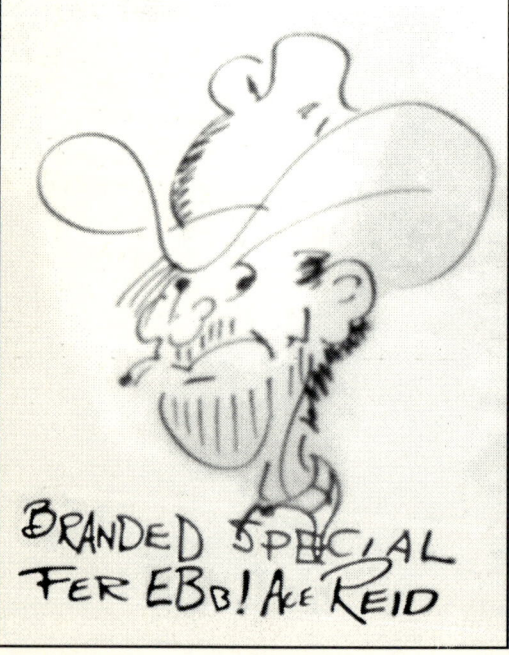

BRANDED SPECIAL
FER EBB! Ace Reid

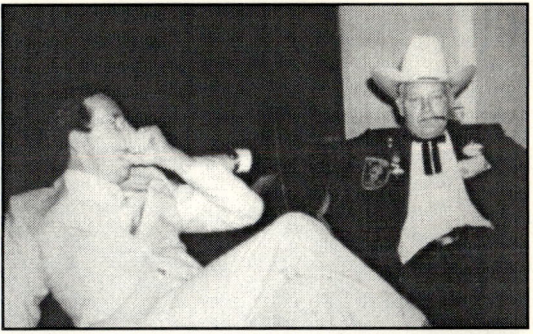
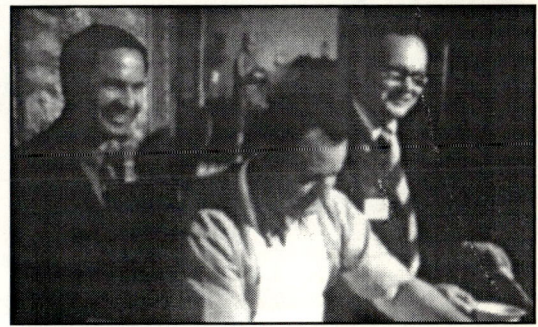

Clockwise from top left: Caricatures of Ebb and Jay
Relaxing with Don Hamilton
Phil Lorfing of the Lowake Steak House hosting a campaigning dinner in Kerrville
Ballinger Lions and their wives at Montreal Convention

(From top)
Other Lion delegations and supporters at the convention in Montreal

Texas delegation at the 1979 convention in Montreal

Family on the stage at the convention

*(From top)
Rickert and
Butler leading
the parade in
Montreal*

*The Six
White Horses
of the Hardin
Simmons
Cowgirls*

*Hardin
Simmons
Cowboy
Band*

(From top) The Doer family, delegates from Fredericksburg

High level political conference, Tex Mayer, Don Buckalew, and Jimmy Pigman

Past International Director Joe Fischer (Senior Federal Judge), Past International President and lawyer Herb Petry, and Ebb

(Top) Ebb talking to Herb Petry at the Inaugural Convention in 1982 in Atlanta, along with Jeff, Michelle, and Jay

(Bottom) Grindstaff & Grindstaff—Judge passes on the gavel to Ebb as president in 1980

*(Clockwise from top right)
President Grindstaff likes to
show off one of his most prized
trophies, this "authentic Texas
Jack-a-lope"*

*Ceremonies and projects in
Sri Lanka*

*Lions in Sri Lanka presenting
mobile equipment to local resident*

Visiting the Taj Mahal

Planning initial International Drug Program with Past International Director Riogone and Executive Secretary Loredona Mandelli

(Above) Jerusalem,
The Dome of the Rock

(Right) Capernaum,
the Tomb of Jesus

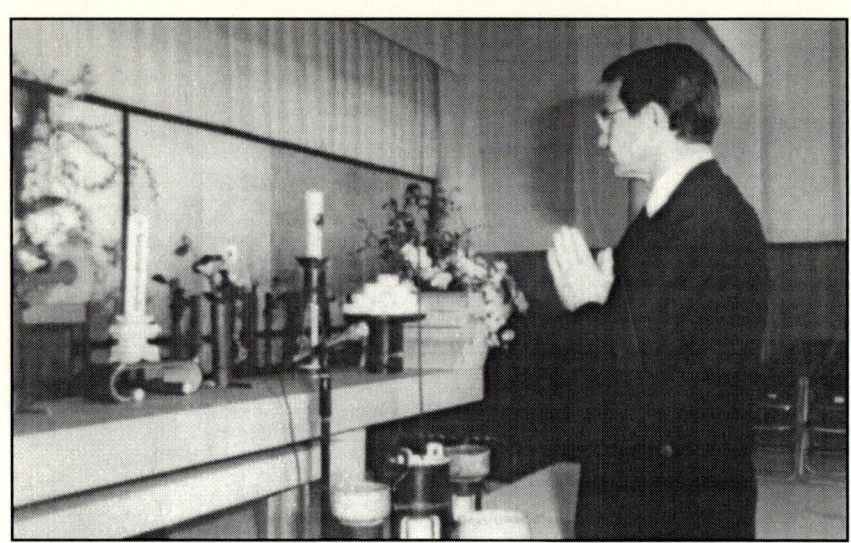

Ebb at the funeral of Past International President Kay Murakami in Kayoto, Japan, in 1983

Gathering sheep in Australia

A ride on the ele-phant in India

(Clockwise from top) Ebb and Jay at the Hadley School for the Blind in Chicago where they met Geraldine Lawhon

Visiting in the home of Iris and Harry Ashcroft in England

Ebb at the Greek Parthenon

Ebb jogging in South Port, England

Meeting with President Belunde in Lima, Peru (a University of Texas graduate)

(Clockwise from top left)
Ebb with Egyptian President
Anwar Sadat at his villa outside Cairo, Egypt, along with
local Lions from Cairo, 1980

Ebb presenting award to
President Zia of Pakistan in
San Francisco

Ebb on camel in Cairo

Prime Minister Begin auto-
graphing book for Ebb at
Jerusalem Conference in 1980

Ebb, Jay, Mr. Dosanni, and
wife from Pakistan

(From top) Jay and Ebb with an audience with Pope John Paul II in St. Peters Square

Ebb with Taiwan President Chiang Ching-Kuo, son of Chiang Kai Chek

Pre-board meeting and visit to Olympic site in Korea, 1981

Everett J. "Ebb" Grindstaff, second left, Immediate Past President of Lions Clubs International, receives the 1983 American Diabetes Association Distinguished Service Award from Joseph H. Davis, left, ADA vice chairman of the board, during the national voluntary health organization's 43rd annual meeting in San Antonio, Texas. Also pictured are ADA board member Past District Governor Dexter Anderson, second right, and Alfred Hodder, president of Medical Alert Foundation International

The Juvenile Diabetes Foundation International awarded its Humanitarian Award to Everett J. "Ebb" Grindstaff, immediate Past President of Lions Clubs International. Grindstaff, pictured here with Todd Dufty, Houston JDF poster boy, and Jacqueline Colville, Past President of JDF International, inaugurated an international Diabetes Education and Awareness Program for Lions Clubs during his 1982-83 presidential term

District 2-Al (my district) Eye Project in Acuna, Mexico, with Past District Governor Paul Palmer, the founder of the project, along with Dr. Stephen Kelly, optomologist from Brownwood to his right, and the local President

Former President Jimmy Carter speaking at 1982 Convention in Atlanta

A dedication of Roy Keaton, Past Director General of Lions Club International from Weatherford, Texas

Ebb with Former President George H. Bush at International Convention in Birmingham, England, 1999

International President Ebb and Jay with President Ronald Reagan and First Lady Nancy, 1983

Ann Landers and Ebb in Chicago participating in the same program at the Lions Convention.

(L-R) Jay, Art Linkletter, Bill Miller, and John Hall in Hawaii

Judge and Art Linkletter at the convention in Hawaii, 1983

Master of Ceremony at Congressman Charles Stenholm's Fun Day

Ebb and Jay with Congressman Charlie Stenholm Dist. 17, Texas, Fun Day and Appreciation Dinner

Weldon Brevard and Grindy in the mountains of Colorado

Ebb and Jay with Family: Michelle, Mark, Tanner and Mackenzie—left Jeff Elizabeth, Will and Kate—right, 2001

Chapter 13

A Lion Leader Goes into Print

The following essays were written by Lion Ebb Grindstaff for the *Abilene Reporter-News*. Some of the material will be repetitive of other parts of the book but are being retained here to preserve the original impact.

Not Sixty Minutes in an Hour

As a practical matter, there are only as many minutes in the hour as you use.

Everyone in the world starts with one thing: the same amount of time. Now the question is what we do with our time. I believe it was Dennis Waitley who described time as being an equal opportunity employer. Rich people can't buy more time, as time is very definitely an equalizer that concerns rich people, paupers, or any individuals in between. Scientists can't invent new minutes, and you can't save time to spend it on another day.

Many, many years ago I read something about the hourglass and I purchased an hourglass and it sits on my desk. It is not used to time my long distance calls, nor to time the boiling of an egg in my office. Nor is it used as a timing device for billing purposes.

If you would turn the hourglass over and watch the thousands of tiny grains of sand tumbling down, you would notice that there is a great deal of activity going on there. Every one of these little grains of sand is on the move. However, if you would observe closely, only one grain of sand at a time can move through the most minute part of the glass. I, too, have many things to do, but this gadget helps me to concentrate on one job until it is properly done.

All of my legal assistants and secretaries that have worked in my office have known this story, and I have been quite shocked at the culprits on occasions when I have been in a fret or buzz and have walked into my office and the hourglass has been turned over to remind me of my own belief and principles.

Our goal should not be how to necessarily find more time because there are limitations, but it should be how to use our time more wisely. Depending on the individual, there is always some credence to the normal statement of "I don't have the time"; however, in the majority of cases this is just one of the many excuses along with the fall season starting, someone else can do it, or if I don't think about it maybe it won't be a problem. There is a time to let things happen and a time to make things happen.

The first step in any type of time trap is, of course, to first recognize the dilemma and then to prioritize our daily course of action. We cannot continue to live at the speed of light and disregard communication and relationships with others. We all start each day with the same opportunity—a time deposit is placed in our life bank each and every day of 1,440 minutes.

Secondly, to everything there is a season and a time to every purpose under Heaven (Ecclesiastes 3:1), which along with the other seven to eight verses graphically portray the different season of time for each of us regardless of our time or station in life.

Today is an important day, and no matter how we spend it, we traded a day of our life for it. It is a gift, but it is up to each of use how we use it. We can squander it, invest it, give it, or lose it, but we can never hoard it. Will we use it wisely?

A Side Trip to "Squaresville"

The late Sen. Margaret Chase Smith (R-Maine) once decried what had happened to the word "square" in her lifetime.

"Many years ago the word square was one of the most honored words in our vocabulary," she once said.

One of America's greatest needs is for more people who are "square."

Are we sweeping ethics under the rug? Is there a need for squares?

To determine whether we are cut out for the nineties, we must ask ourselves the following: Is ethics fashionable? Do I take ethics seriously? Do I understand ethical conduct?

What disturbs me the most is the antagonism and conflict among Americans.

The absence of ethics is fashionable in political offices, campaign contributions, governmental positions, savings and loan associations, college athletics programs, local government positions, religion, and TV ministries. In fact, I know of no profession (unfortunately including my own) or vocation that has not been scarred.

Ethics is and should be one of the most timely subjects in this, the threshold decade of the twenty-first century. Even though we are sitting in the front seat of one of the most exhilarating and exciting decades in the century, it appears we do not know the meaning of the word ethics, nor do we know the application of ethics in our everyday life.

However, ethics has been fashionable for thousands of years.

Ethics is even a global word as it comes from the Greek word "ethos" for character. Plato and Aristotle thought that ethical conduct was virtuous conduct and that the practice of virtuous conduct would build character.

Harvard Business Review defines ethics, as used in conversation, as "a set of moral principles or values to guide behavior." Therefore, ethical behavior is the behavior that conforms to these values, to moral and basic principles.

We will not take ethics seriously until we care for other people. How? By respecting the human dignity and the worth of each individual. The real problem is not knowing what is right or wrong but in doing what is right or wrong.

What is the practical meaning of ethics? I believe that there is one value, one core word that holds all other values together—integrity.

We have all heard the adage that honesty is the best policy, but actually honesty needs to be a way of life.

There was a time when people dealt from an ethical base in their lives, but things began to change for the worst, and unethical behavior became more common, even applauded. Integrity is something that must be thought of as a valuable commodity.

It is time to sound the alarm. However, it will depend on each of us as individuals.

The greatest speech that I ever heard consisted of ten two-letter words: "If it is to be, it is up to me."

Are you willing to be that one?

Leadership from Servants

Unfortunately, in the last decade or two, most people have associated greatness with coercive power. However, greatness is really synonymous with service.

To equate greatness, you must really associate it with humbling oneself or shifting a person's fulfillment of self or inward desires to that of serving others, whether it be business, family, or community. Rather than to associate leadership with the ability to control the action of others, there is a desperate need for servant leaders. Why do people back away from the word "servant" or "service to others"?

A servant leader really has a vision of what other people desire and want most and does not necessarily equate the position to power but to a contribution of self.

There is no question that volunteerism is again in the limelight, and it is even being required by a host of business corporations and firms. People don't want to be managed. They want to be led. Like your horse. You can lead your horse to water, but you can't manage him to drink.

Napoleon, like any wise leader, was aware that his own success would have been nothing had his men not been willing, even eager, to follow him. Helping others to achieve their goals —that's the essence of leadership.

It will not work if a leader walks into the position and says he is going to be your leader, you are to follow him, and if you do not do this then look out. A rare kind of leadership, servant leadership, will be required. We can look at all the leaders in those particular businesses and see they are really servant leaders who seek power only as something held in trust to be used for the benefit of all people, not something which one possesses only to be reinvested in further power.

We need leaders that understand that one governs by example as much as one governs by programs. Even though I did not vote for Ross Perot in the presidential election, I would quickly admit that I liked some of the words espoused that at least focused on service to others instead of self.

For the first time in our history we are challenged with a global society demanding leaders who are willing to serve. As president of Lions Clubs International I had the opportunity to meet with many of the presidents, prime ministers, and other leaders of different countries (having the wonderful opportunity to travel in more than fifty free countries in one year) and my observation of the traits of these leaders was that each was not only a humble person but believed in returning to basics, caring for people, and responding to change—and most of all in serving others.

The protection and dignity of human life in the twenty-first century depends on individuals and companies who are willing to return to being serving leaders, who believe in a meaningful, value clarification system. Yes, individuals can make a difference.

A young boy was sitting with his dad late one summer evening while fishing.

The boy, observing the lightning bugs flicking around, asked his dad how the bugs were able to light up. The father, engrossed in his own thinking or entranced by the fishing, failed to answer. The young boy then reached out and caught one of the bugs between the palms of his hands.

The boy looked down, saw no light, and then turned to his

dad and said, "Now I know what makes the light. It's the stuff inside." The stuff inside is the core of servant leadership.

Inability to Communicate

"Giving folgidi-aoc"
The above letters are an indication of one of the greatest problems that we have in America today—the inability to communicate.

Of all the advances made in science and technology, I am concerned about the development of the greatest computer that has ever been made or ever will be made—the human mind.

Dr. Jonas Salk says that the last frontier that we have to conquer in America is the human mind, which means that we must have development of human relationships, of sharing information, of good communication essential to the survival of the human species.

We must get away from the quest for materialism and strive for the intangible peace of mind that comes from the development of stable human relationships.

In more than thirty years as a lawyer, the core of marital breakup, parent-child relationships, family disputes, and, yes, even broken contracts or other type of agreements is a lack of communication.

Did you see the cartoon? Man sitting at breakfast table with a cup of coffee, newspaper in front of him, glasses on; wife is standing before him in a sweater, hair uncombed, looking as if she had arisen too early. The husband asks: "What do you mean we don't communicate? Didn't you get my fax yesterday?"

Communication takes many forms and is not only just the written word. For instance, a smile increases our face value.

Actually, a failure to communicate is a misnomer because everything that we do communicates something. The way we look or act, or don't look or act speaks clearly to those you encounter.

Linda Paulson, in her book *The Executive Persuader,* relates that failure to communicate is not an option. As she tells her clients, "You cannot not communicate."

What we are communicating is either positive or negative, and contributes to or detracts, enhances or diminishes, but a message always comes through. Peter Drucker, management guru, states that sixty percent of all management problems are caused by poor communication. He relates that he saw a sign attached to a high-voltage transformer that simply read: "Test this and you're fried"—a well-communicated message.

When Coca-Cola first began to market its product in China, it did so using a phonetic version of its brand name, Koo-kah-koo-lah. Sales dropped, and nobody could figure out why until someone pointed out that, when translated, Koo-kah-koo-lah meant "bite the wax tadpole." Sales rose dramatically, however after Coca-Cola made a slight change to Kah-Koo-kah-lah, which means "may the happy mouth rejoice."

Many of today's heroes send mixed communications about right and wrong.

Certain rock stars or professional athletes are obviously successful in their careers and enjoy great wealth, yet their lifestyles may include drug use.

Business leaders, even government officials, may be seen on the nightly news, having been indicated for graft or other illegal activities. Sometimes the wrong messages are communicated.

If you have three frogs on a log and one frog decides to jump, how many do you have left? You still have three. One frog decided to jump, but it is not enough to make a decision if you do not act.

Will you be the one to act and more effectively communicate in all facets of your life?

The Value of Grass-Roots Living

A very rare breed of people live in West Texas. Only certain individuals have the faith and patience to depend on the elements for rain to quench our thirst, to provide moisture for crops, and to enjoy the beauty of West Texas vegetation.

As we observe every year the first leaves of the mesquite and see the first grass roots spring upward, we realize our faith and patience have again been rewarded. For this reason, grass roots has been a term of endearment for this area.

The significance dawned on me while listening to a good friend, Gen. Robbie Risner, describe his some seven years as a POW in Vietnam—fifty-four months of his confinement spent in isolation, ten months in total darkness. You can imagine that he was under intense physical and mental stress.

One morning at daylight after a particularly frustrating day, Robbie got down on the floor of his seven-foot-by-seven-foot cell and crawled under the bunk where there was a vent in the floor that allowed in fresh air from the outside.

He saw a faint glimmer of light reflected on the inside of the vent. Being curious, he put his eye next to the cement wall and discovered a minute crack in the construction to see outside.

The hole was so small that all he could see was a single blade of grass. One ray of light, one single blade of grass. But it represented life, growth, freedom, and knowledge that God had not forgotten him. Grass roots living.

Since my appointment to the Upper Colorado River Authority in 1960, the term Stacy Lake served as a dream and a hope for West Texas for drinking water—grass roots for present and future generations. It is a very high honor to serve on the Upper Colorado River Authority for twenty-nine years, seventeen years as chairman, being appointed by Governor Price Daniel, Governor Preston Smith, Governor Bill Clements and Governor Mark White.

Time after time I had watched the flood waters of Elm Creek and Colorado River flow through Ballinger on the way to its final destination—the Gulf of Mexico. What a waste that seemed.

My dream continued until finally, through the leadership of the Colorado River Municipal Water District and the tenacity of Owen Ivie and many individuals too numerous to mention, the dream became a reality.

The icing on the cake was the early filling of the reservoir to its capacity of more than 550,000 acre feet in less than two years. It will ensure drinking water for the cities and towns of the large expanse of West Texas, as well as a beautiful body of water which provides recreation for thousands.

Stacy (now O.H. Ivie) Lake is the epitome of grass-roots

people who have the tenacity to overcome unfounded objections from the south (in fact, Stacy prevented flood damage in a large area), special interest groups, and, yes, even the Concho Water Snake to make a dream come true.

Now we must use and further develop this area. What is of benefit to one city or town in this part of West Texas is of benefit to the entire area.

Instead of trying to add years to life in the chaotic pursuit of material things, we need to add life to years by appreciating the beauty of God's creative work and the quality of grass-roots living.

A Return to 'Quail Values'

Do you feel that you are living at the speed of light? We have been living with personal computers, microwaves, fax machines, and cash in a flash, and are moving into the age of video telephone (cuts out a lot of talking in the bathroom), filmless cameras, robotics, laser, hyprosonic airplanes, levitated magnetic trains traveling over 300 mph, pills that will increase your memory four hundred percent (really looking forward to this one).

But there is one intricate gadget that still gives me a problem—the greatest computer that has ever been built—that of the human mind, which is necessary for the establishment of stable human relationships. In fact, Dr. Jonas Salk says the last frontier in America that we have to conquer is the human mind.

Regardless of position, politics, or power, respect should be granted for the concept of belief in, return to, or the misplacement of values. This is true even of it is Vice President Dan Quayle, whom I at least respect for his position on values, as such.

But I thought it should be reduced to a common denominator familiar to us grassroots folks in West Texas-Quail Values.

The consequences of the use of certain words, names, or phrases is sometimes subject to controversy. However, the scope of our thoughts and hopes for the future of this and coming generations depends on the return of, continuation of, or change of basic values for a quality life.

Our nation is in the clutches of a moral crisis. The Josephson Institute for the Advancement of Ethics says we belong to a generation that is less anchored in bedrock ethical values than any other.

The price tags that reflect our sense of values have all gotten mixed up. People major on minor things and minor on major things. Further, we love things and use people instead of loving people and using things.

It isn't enough to have principles in a written program or constitution. They must be in the heart and soul.

Individual human spirit comes first. It is our wellspring of strength, the spirit of democracy.

The entertainment industry, among others, promotes every form of sexual adventurism and graphic brutality glorifying vicious characters who treat killing as a joke. The nation's history, its future, and its major institutions are viewed as dark, cynical, and often nightmarish, while vulgar behavior, contempt for all abilities, and obscene language are celebrated.

Now, the good news. Nearly all trend forecasters and polls show materialism on the decline and the increasing importance of all values, including family.

Faith Popcorn, one of the leading forecasters in the United States, calls the nineties the S.O.S. decade—save our society— the decency decade. The return to land, religion, family, values, simplicity. The decade dedicated to three E's—environment, education, ethics. No more of the "me generation."

We need to change the Golden Rule from the practicality of the last few years—"Do unto others first so they won't get it done unto you"—back to the original: Do unto others that you would also like done unto you.

Only, we—you and me and grass-roots people—can make a difference, regardless of our jobs, profession or position in life. Doing good is no longer an option. It is a must—a return to the basic values of life.

If you desire to enrich days, plant seeds. If you desire to enrich years, plant trees. If you desire to enrich lives, plant ideals and ideas. Ebb Grindstaff is a Ballinger attorney. He is one of twenty-one members of the *Reporter-News'* board of contributors.

Chapter 14

Learn to Speak Effectually

To present any speech, you need to prepare.

You need to prepare your subject matter, and you need to prepare to make sure that you emphasize and get over the point or points that you intend. Never try to get over too many points in one speech because it is certainly more emphatic if you can get over a couple of points in an able and clear manner.

I always use humor and/or illustrations, depending upon the crowd—most of the time at the beginning because I want to make a connection with the crowd.

You should be able to tell quickly whether a group responds to humor, and you can increase or decrease the humor content depending on early reactions.

Illustrations are mainly used to make a particular point. I've always found that the audience reacts better to speakers who have illustrations or a signature story and use them in such a manner that listeners will respond to and remember the point.

In a large crowd, it is difficult to make connections with one, five, or ten individuals, and I've tried to look over the top of the crowd—barely—because I still want to think that I'm speaking to each and every individual. And that should be the prime motivation: to make each person in that audience think

123

you are speaking to him or her. Sometimes it helps to connect eye-to-eye and tends to make the whole group feel you are sharing attention. I have used this effectively on groups of 500 to 600 and larger.

In a smaller audience, it is mandatory that you make contact—even for just a few seconds, without jumping around like a chicken with its head cut off to another individual or section of the audience. This is one reason it is necessary to have your speech or your outline in order so you can refer back to your outline if necessary.

I always try to have my speech or outline in mind and—on most occasions—I'm prepared enough that I don't need to refer to them even though the outline and/or notes are handy.

My dad taught me that you should always be scared or concerned before making any speech, because if you are not you won't make a good one.

Visual aids can be appropriate as the old proverb says: "One picture is worth ten thousand words." In most instances, it is not practical for me to use the visual—except in some of the training sessions in Lion's Clubs International, but is always recommended by the National Speakers Association and its affiliates.

One of my favorite short versions of a good speech was "What's Your Point" by Bob Boyland, but a lot of my speech training came from declamation in high school and debate in college (under Glenn Capp at Baylor, a nationally recognized debate professor).

One of the most astounding men I have ever known was in the drama department at Baylor University. His name is Paul Baker. He later left Baylor over a disagreement on some dialogue in a play production, but I took a drama class under him while I was in law school and reaped great benefits. I will always remember Baker told me that I would affect audiences and juries because of my sincere, honest approach and my genuineness.

Judge Abner McCall was another mentor who taught me to be humble, forthright, and short in speeches.

Another mentor in the professional speech industry was Kay Baker from Austin, who not only heard me speak but listened to several of my tapes. She was a tremendous mentor and helped develop outlines, speeches, brochures, tapes, materials, and philosophy, spending hours and days on this project. Kay has been active in local, regional, and the national chapters of the National Speakers Association, serving as president of the regional and director of the national association. Kay has presented speeches to many types of governmental and business groups and many other types of business organizations. Kay was a West Texas girl from Fort Stockton and spent all of her professional life in Austin.

She said my reaction to the situation in hand or the people or being able to work them into the speech with a personal touch was one of my greater assets.

On the area of the talk, you may stand behind the podium for the entire time, but do not appear to be stiff or immovable—you need to show some reaction to the people. On some occasions with a mobile microphone, you can move about and make even better contact than from behind the podium.

My most difficult speeches would be those probably in southern Europe, Morocco, Tunisia, and all the French-speaking countries. I had to have an interpreter and use illustrations—which was not the best because I could have used other means.

I'll never forget the French interpreter going over one of my stories that he had heard before. We went over it three or four times, and then he translated it and it still didn't come out as if I had been talking. I would sometimes cut my speeches a lot shorter in South America, and even shorter in Japan—though I had been stationed in Japan for a year and lived there for a year. All I had to do was use a few Japanese words from my days in Japan and I was popular. I don't believe they cared what you said, as long as you were there and because you were an officer or president of Lion's Club International.

I have made thousands of speeches—often for different groups for similar occasions. But even though I have given a similar speech before, I still prepare and go over it as if it were a new speech. But in those situations when they seem too overwritten or fixed, I try to bring in the audience and relate to them. If I learn something about the group or an individual from the head table, I take advantage of it by sharing it with the crowd.

I often use code words—or key words—in speech outlines.

Sometimes it isn't easy to remember the connection because it could have been noted from years ago.

The best idea is to try to have an outline with some code or key words that you can just glance down and jog your memory without appearing to be reading. I've never read a speech like some of the politicians or other speakers do at a meeting, unless it's a new place and there is absolutely no time to prepare; but even then I try to have the "jist" of it in my mind.

If I'm giving a twenty-five-minute speech, I'll try to jot down a few ideas during the time of introduction and other parts of the program and try to bring them into the speech. If I'm familiar with the material, the key words may be no more than a few letters long—just in case I get so enthused with what I'm talking about that I forget it.

I often use the initials "TGAL" which is for "Think Globally and Act Locally." I first used that philosophy—one of my favorites—in 1981 before it became very popular in the late eighties and early nineties.

But speaking is one of the many areas in which it helps to be a Lion.

The Lion's program is a training source, even locally and for the local officers—especially for the local president. Some of them may never have addressed a public meeting before and they are naturally scared or concerned for whatever the reasons might be.

I remember our district governor some forty years ago, who was a marvelous individual, but on his first official visit he could hardly speak. He was so scared and afraid that he wouldn't do a good job. But twelve months later, he could stand up and give a good, down-to-earth speech.

In Lion's Club International, in the United States and Canada, they have a USA-Canadian forum—which is over twenty years old—that is a training session for the individual Lions; they encourage the grass-root Lions to attend these sessions. They always have three or four international performers, motivators, or those who give inspiration.

I made the arrangments to have Zig Ziglar as the keynote performer at our USA-Canadian forum in Calgary. Because of health problems, I could not attend that particular weekend, which was very disapppointing as I had read three or four of his books and heard three or four of his tapes and also had the opportunity to hear him on other occasions. The Lions thought he was really the "top of the line."

LaDonna Gatlin, the yougest of the singing Gatlin kids, was in Tucson, Arizona, for a Lions forum, and a few months later in Austin with brother Rudy from Dallas along with her folks—what a talented family—who lived in Ballinger for a short time, but spent much of their time in Odessa where Mr. Gatlin was involved in the oil field.

The forums are held once a year—usually in thc fall—and the international convention is usually around July 4th. They have a humanitarian award that is given out each year in the form of cash—which has now risen to some $150,000 to $200,000 for the particular cause or charity with which the honoree is working.

Art Linkletter received the Humanitarian Award in 1983 when I presided at the convention in Honolulu, Hawaii. Mother Theresa received the Humanitarian Award. Past President Jimmy Carter was also a recipient of the award for his work with Habitat for Humanity. In fact, the Lion's Club International has joined with his organization to further this effort not only in America, but in South America as well.

In 1982, when I was president of the Lion's Club, I introduced the Diabetes and Drug Awareness as international programs because they were subjects that applied throughout the world—the diabetic program because diabetes is the leading cause of new blindness. Now that program has developed into research and the "Sight First" campaign has raised some $175 million.

The Lions' Drug Awareness program has grown into the Quest Program for educating young children. Both of these programs are still active, even after twenty years.

We also presented the Journey for Sight program—which was to be a fundraiser for Lion's Clubs International, and it went over well.

We thought about naming it "Run for Sight" or "Jog for Sight" because I was a jogger, but we decided on the name "Journey" because that included running, walking, and other modes. We ended up having dogsled races, scooter races, snow sled races, bike races, three-wheeled races (in India), and different kinds of races throughout the world, and it seemed to acquire great acclaim.

In the Drug Program, the Lions of Texas in 1978-1981 had been very active in a statewide program on the fight against drugs, and it was a pleasure for me to introduce that internationally. In 1969-1971, when I was president of the Crippled Children's Camp, we started the diabetic program for juvenilles and went into partnership with a South Texas Diabetic Association—Dr. Travis and his group—and started the Diabetic Camp for juveniles in Kerrville in 1971. We worked that in with the Crippled Children's Camp.

In 1949 the Lion's Club acquired land—over 200 acres—from the government for the camps. In 1953 they began the camp with the first camping session—which coincided with the outbreak of polio. We did have a program for the blind during the winter off-season for several years during the 1960s, but it eventually ended; and in 1971 we were looking for a new field of service, and that was when we started the program for juvenile diabetics.

Speakers shouldn't digress too much, so back to elements of effectual speaking.

I've always appreciated constructive criciticism, such as some notes in a critique from 1989: Chin up. Eye contact. Slow down, slow down—talk again when you feel pain. Pause, pause, pause makes a point. Be dramatic . . . Practice, practice, practice using a soft voice, but still projecting. Tie-in, tie-in, tie-in points to illustrations.

In the nineties, I was a member of the North Texas Professional Speaker's Association and also the South Texas Professional Speaker's Association. I even produced some tapes and also a video and learned through those organizations how to do a critique of a tape or video and/or from memory. During that period of time, I had an occasion to critique myself and also have someone like Kay Baker critique along with David Byrd (a very talented individual from Beeville via University of Texas in Austin), who also helped me to develop a video.

Juanell Teague, a partner of mine from Dallas helped me

to develop a brochure and the information necessary for dissemination to the general public. However, between making speeches for the Lions and having to again practice law, I was not able to follow through with this in the manner that I would have liked.

Zig Ziglar was one of my motivators in life and, as a communicator, made several suggestions that I actually used in the past. Even though I had espoused some of these basics, I had only written down some of these thoughts from seminars that I attended and in making speeches, books, and videos that I had consumed. I even attended four or five of his Sunday school classes in downtown First Baptist Church in Dallas, where he performed with the same zest and enthusiasm. I believe he said that you can have everything in life you want if you have enough people get what they want in life—not as a tactic, but as a matter of human nature. Some of his advice:

1. Relax and feel good about yourself;

2. Present a speech on a seventh grade level. (And many of his speeches always had a break for humor, such as saying that every third person is handsome, now look to the right and now look to the left);

3. Women are very practical, both in their approaches and in their recipe for material (for instance, the bum asked the woman on the street if she would give a dollar for a sandwich, and the woman said, no, not until I see the sandwich);

4. Many people (including myself at various times depending upon the audience) always use humor in the beginning, because if you can get the audience to relax and feel good about themselves, they will feel good about you. Whatever you use, the beginning should be a profound story, experience, or development. At some stage you shift gears from the humorous to the more serious, but still feel comfortable and have fun, and explain the benefits of their attending;

5. Determine the reason that you are there and the message that you are to convey. You are either there to entertain—or if it is more formal, you are there to motivate and you need to move the audience into action;

6. If you use other material from other sources (which is sat-

isfactory), you should certainly give them credit, as it shows that you have researched the subject, and it's the right thing to do;

7. Be optimistic. One example: Ziglar always said people normally are of a negative nature—the golfer who tees off with the lake in front, and the ball goes in the lake, and he says, "I knew I was going to do that." The audience is from a negative world, and we get the opportunity to lift them up and give them a zest for life. Of course, life is tough, and speaking is tough;

8. Many of the ideas that various speakers use as a method were ideas that I had previously used in life and speaking, but it did confirm some of these practices; however, a lot of these ideas were espoused by others: Lewis Timberlake, Kay Baker, Elizabeth Brazell, and many other speakers of the South Texas and North Texas Speakers' Association. I attended meetings and conventions of both these groups for several years in order to hone my speaking presentations. The people in these meetings were professionally paid speakers, top of the line, and presented their speeches to the particular occasion for which they were speaking, and did a magnificent job. I guess some of the better advice was if you could take three lessons from a golf pro and go on the circuit, everybody would be on the circuit. The same thing with a speaker, if you could take three lessons and go on the circuit, everybody would be on the circuit; but it would not be as lucrative and not as professional.

They all said that you must *learn,* you must *practice,* you must *learn,* you must *practice,* etc. There's a difference between a workaholic and a peak performer. A workaholic performs out of fear or grief and a peak performer performs out of love and emotion.

Summary of typical suggestions for speakers:

1. Words paint the pictures even though one picture is worth 10,000 words;
2. Watch your language;
3. Use words of hope and encouragement;
4. Every nine to eleven minutes make an effort to make your audience laugh;
5. Use logic;
6. Use emotion;

7. Use instruction;

8. Use inspiration;

9. Use parable—the greatest teacher;

10. Tell stories;

11. Make every speech as if it were your last speech;

12. Prepare physically, spiritually, and mentally;

13. Prepare, Practice, Learn, Prepare, Practice, Learn;

14. Even if you are making the same speech for the one thousandth time, you must act as if it were opening night—and it will be for somebody;

15. Improve your speech every time you deliver it;

16. What you say to people can make a dramatic difference in their life;

17. Live your speech—if you're excited, notify your face;

18. One thing people look for is genuineness;

19. It's the little things that make the difference;

20. You must have something to say;

21. You must say it well;

22. Be yourself;

23. Use your own personal experiences;

24. Use humorous stories;

25. Dress impeccably;

26. Always use correct grammar;

27. Establish your uniqueness;

28. Research and prepare your own material;

29. Have quality.

There have been at least three outstanding past presidents in Lions Clubs International who are outstanding speakers: Past President Dick Bryan from Ohio and Arizona, who was appointed to my board in 1982-1983 and who presented seminars and training sessions for years for Goodyear Tire Company in Ohio and many other states (in addition thereto, he presented the same types of programs in Lions Clubs International and also has been a very popular speaker for conventions, anniversaries and other programs); Judge Brian Stevenson, who served as president in 1987-88, and is one of the senior judges of the Criminal Trial Division of Provincial Court in Alberta, a position he had held for twenty-two years as of this writing; Past President

Bill Biggs, a lawyer from Nebraska who has spoken at many district governor elect seminars and opening sessions and also has been very popular as a speaker because of his enthusiasm and zeal for the subject matter he presents and without being too lengthy in his presentation. In addition, Brian was chairman of the fundraising arm of the Sightfirst, which raised some $175 million for this project. His leadership will be known through the years. Brian and I have shared information and have talked about speaking skills on many occasions, and he has written an article in Lions Club magazine, which had to be divided into three parts and is very explicit as to the do's and don'ts of speaking. I am going to share just a bit of this information with you, mostly quotes and jokes, with Brian's permission, as so many of the points included have already been referred to in some form or fashion.

For successful speaking skills you need to write your speech at least three times.

We both agree with Daniel Webster who said, "If all my possessions and powers were to be taken from me with one exception, and I could choose that exception, I would choose to keep the power of speech, for by it I could soon recover all the rest."

Communicate, Communicate, Communicate; that cannot be said too often. Even in the legal profession, we attempt to present our cases for the court in easily understood English.

Bad examples of comunication:

Q. Who was your wife before you were married?
A. I don't recall having a wife then.
Q. And you admit to having committed adultery?
A. Yes.
Q. With someone other than your wife?
A. Is there another way?

Kids often get confused. In New York, a sixth-grader wrote an essay on adults. In part, this is what he had to say: "Adults don't do anything. Adults just sit around and talk and don't do a thing. There's not anything duller in the world than adultery."

Another youngster explained the thought process as follows: "When we think, the brain gets all electrocuted. But that don't hurt because we don't feel nothing up there anyhow."

A very serious fifth grade student displayed an interest in becoming a doctor when he wrote these words in his health class: "Standing on your legs is dangerous. Standing on your legs too long causes very close veins."

One of the rules mentioned above is open your eyes and minds, as was done at the International Convention in July of 1996 in Montreal, in one of the greatest openings of all times by the first words of President Jimmy Carter, a Lion, "It's a long way from the office of Tail Twister to the office of president in the United States."

The lack of communication can be exemplified by a few quotes from church bulletins:

"This afternoon, there will be baptismal meetings in the south and north ends of the church. Children will be baptized at both ends."

"Thursday, at 5:00 P.M., there will be a meeting of the little mother's club. All those wishing to become little mothers will please meet with the minister in his study."

"This being Easter Sunday, we will ask Mrs. Brown to come forward and lay an egg on the altar."

"In the future the preacher for the following Sunday will be found hanging on the bulletin board."

"Don't let worry kill you; let the church help."

For example, this sign appeared on the door of a dentist's office in Hong Kong:

"Teeth Extracted By Latest Methodists."

This caution was posted in a hotel in Tokyo: "It Is Forbidden To Steal Hotel Towels. If You Are Not A Person To Do Such A Thing, Please Do Not Read This Notice."

At a hotel in Leipzig, Germany, this translation was posted by the elevator: "Do Not Enter The Lift Backwards, And Only When Lit Up."

Back in Hong Kong, this advisory appeared in a tailor shop: "Ladies May Have A Fit Upstairs."

Danish passengers checking in at Copenhagen Airlines may be understandably worried by this sign: "We Take Your Bags And Send Them In All Directions."

Bottom line: communicate with your audience with clear and understandable English.

Chapter 15

Families Are the Be-All and End-All

Families are probably the most important aspect of our lives in America because of our early heritage and because of the values that we must perceive as a child, or the values that we must teach. I guess the priority of my parents was the church and education. Values, integrity, and honesty were hammered into my head over and over again until it became so foremost in my mind that it should simply be a way of life. It should be something accepted, and it should be something that people do.

In the 1930s, 40s, and 50s, that's the way it was. People even executed contracts between each other on a handshake rather than some written words that lawyers might sit down and have people execute. Those contracts were valid and dependable because people had faith and integrity with whom they were dealing.

The next one would have to be a work ethic. This is something my parents taught by example; they were not rich, they were not poor. Both of their parents said you had to earn what you worked for, and you had to work long and hard and in an honest manner to do that.

Of course, my early teachings were from two teachers. Both

Judge and Mimi were teachers. They both taught me so much and set so many examples by both of the lives they lived with their participations in Sunday school and in church, in the school system, and in the community.

Of course, being the only child, and having both parents that worked back in the 1940s was a little bit unusual; so on Saturday—and even during the week—it was my shift to mow the lawn and to do some of the kitchen chores such as washing the dishes, dusting, mopping, cooking, etc. They did not have time to do it all. But I had some other buddies who had to do that also, so I did not feel quite as bad.

It was the work ethic and integrity that were attributes of both sets of grandparents, because they worked long and hard. They did their best to see that their children had a better life than they did. Mimi set many examples and especially encouraged me to study and make good grades and to be the best in all that I did.

Even though I participated in many athletic activities, I did not necessarily excel. I did win doubles at district in tennis, and on to regionals. At 152 pounds, Jimmy Gresset and I were probably the best two tackle reserves for a 260-pound tackle, Alton Patterson and 220-pound Muleshoe Wallace. I also participated in basketball and in the band as a clarinet player.

I enjoyed all the participation of debate to athletics to drama and other school activities. So I have to give credit to Mimi for her encouragement and participation, along with Judge who encouraged me in speech and other activities.

They both encouraged me in the law, as I never had any other idea except that I would be a lawyer, and I always had plans to go to the University of Texas, like Judge did in the summer. I had already registered and Bob Agnew and I were going to be roommates. But the summer before I was scheduled to start at UT, I visited the Baylor campus when we were on a trip to the east coast. I thought it was the friendliest campus, with a Christian background and a smaller school than Texas—Baylor being around 5,000 and Texas 20,000 then.

Bob Agnew was my closest neighbor, and his mom Treva was like another mother to me, and I played golf with Mr. Agnew, who is a good golfer just as his son Bob turned out to be.

It was only a month or so before the finalization of this book that Bob Agnew (whose wife Betty Lou was a Ballingerite and a long-time friend), Walter Hill (whose wife Jackie was a native of Paint Rock and we double dated together two or three years), and Hal (Dizz) Caskey (whose wife Judy is from Lueders and is a tough survivor of two or three years of cancer at this writing), along with myself—all of whom started the first grade together in Ballinger—got together for a foursome reunion in Granbury and then to golf at Glen Rose. There is nothing like friends from grade school who have kept up with each other and have had successful careers in their own right.

I think that Ballinger natives have seemed to be more successful than other towns. We've had doctors, engineers, other professionals, in all facets of life; in addition, we've had leaders in different associations as Aubrey Faubion was president of one of the farm dealers associations of the state of Texas; Darrell Rains was president of the Funeral Homes Directors Association; Jerry Willingham is a state leader in the insurance association; there are numerous others in the education field, such as Morris Sweeney, a chemistry teacher in Ballinger for many years, and Grant Lee. Both were science teachers, and many other graduates from these two teachers were successful in all fields and especially in science and the production of many medical doctors as the result of Grant Lee's teachings.

Speaking of outstanding graduates, we had to pull for Texas Tech for several years because Spike Dykes, a Ballinger native, was a successful coach at Texas Tech, and we had the opportunity to go to several of the games and sit in his box, which we thoroughly enjoyed. At the Baylor homecoming games we are usually on the goal line. We have a good friend and ex-star basketball player and his wife who obtain the tickets—John and LaNell Starkey. In 2001 they decided to change the method after over forty years, and we had good tickets anyway on the opposite end of the Baylor stadium on the goal line. Spike Dykes, who married a Ballinger native and close family friend, Sharon Tuckey, and Weldon Brevard, who married Diane Wilson, also a Ballinger native and close friend, went to nearly all of the Texas Tech games, and we always rode with them to those games. Weldon and Spike were both on that famous 1953 state championship finalist football team, the only time Ballinger went to the state finals (we had some great, great teams in the 1940s—during the tenure of Pooch Wright and later on, Bob Wright— but at that particular time you could go no further than the regionals). Their coach was Doug Cox (Cox as a player and Dykes as a coach were inducted into the Texas Football Hall of Fame). Cox is one of my twenty-year doubles tennis partners—along with the original four, Doug Cox, Doug Wadsworth, Rodney Gordon, and myself, and later Jimmy Dankworth, Bob McDaniel, and Mike White.

I was very fortunate, as I could not ask for any better support all during my growing years and even after I graduated from high school and law school and thereafter. I had actually thought about going to Weatherford after I graduated from law school (or at least after I got out of the service). I had two great uncles who were lawyers (and inspirations for Judge). There was Uncle Lige, who practiced in Weatherford, and Uncle Henry, who practiced in Haskell, Rotan, and Roby. Uncle Lige ran a successful practice and firm at that particular time, but I knew the Judge had always wanted me to practice in Ballinger, and I also had in mind the possibility of running for state representative, which I could have done in Ballinger at that time.

After I married Jay and became acquainted with her family, we found out we had another very supportive group. It was unusual that during all their lifetimes my folks and Jay's folks truly enjoyed being with each other and shared common interests; we spent holidays and Christmases together, and it sure did save a lot of arguments.

The first time I met Albert White, Sr., Jay's dad in Fort Worth, Albert, Jr. was younger and still in high school, and I do not think he had even thought of becoming a lawyer at that time. Albert, Sr. asked me the question (hardly before I could say hello) as to if I could be a Christian and a lawyer at the same time. I don't even know what I said at the time (even though I did indicate that I could or I would not have been pursing that particular vocation unless I also could be a Christian), but Albert and Ruth both had strong Christian backgrounds, coming from Alabama, via Arkansas, to Fort Worth, Texas.

Mr. White was postmaster in Lepanto in Arkansas, where

Jay was born and spent seven years of her life, and then later studied music education, was in the contracting business, and in the fundraising business for churches and educational institutions. They were both active in Sunday school and outreach in the Gamble Street Baptist Church in Fort Worth, where we were married. In fact, during one of the first fundraising activities in 1958, the Ballinger Memorial Hospital was to receive $250,000 in the Hill-Burton funds for the building of the hospital, and Ballinger needed to raise another $250,000 in matching funds. The Whites were hired, came to town, and were successful in their venture of raising funds and providing healthcare to the citizens of Ballinger and the surrounding areas at that time for all these years.

Mary Eleanor White Sanders was the oldest of the three White children. Early on she married her high school beau, Jim Sanders, who worked for the Southwestern Bell telephone company. At retirement, they moved to the Albert, Jr., ranch and spent their retirement years. Jim passed away in July of 2001. They had four girls who had various careers, families, and businesses.

Albert, Jr., was a star basketball player from Paschal High School in Fort Worth and later played basketball for the Baylor Bears; it was during those years that he met Mary Jane Cowden from Pearsall. Albert, Jr. also went to Baylor Law School; he was in the army for two years, returned to Fort Worth and became assistant city attorney, worked for a well-known defense law firm, and then was elected district judge where he served for a number of years until his retirement. Then he served as a mediator and as a visiting judge, which allowed him to spend more time at the ranch, his first love. Albert and Mary Jane had three children, Coleman, Albert White III (Trey)—a Baylor graduate —and Molly, who went to Baylor one year then transferred to A&M.

Jay and I basically had the same set of values, ones we had acquired both at home and Baylor University. We attempted to instill those same values in our children and grandchildren. We have been most fortunate in having two lovely children, and of course four of the smartest, most intelligent, most beautiful, most handsome, caring, loving grandchildren that you could have. That is not to say that we have not had ups and downs at various times in upbringing. That is when our values were put to the test to face our own shortcomings and our desire for our children; and thereafter, our patience and our unfailing love and understanding for each other proved strong.

Jay and I had two children: Jeff, who was born July 1, 1956, and Michelle, who was born January 6, 1959. We were back in the states on March 29, 1956, from Japan. We would have to say that Jeff had his initial beginning in Japan. Jeff was always pretty good sized, and was six feet, two hundred pounds when he was a senior in high school and made all-district football. However, he had no particular desire to pursue the possibilities of college football. Jeff was always interested in agriculture and the farm, and we went through the pig-raising bit, but basically we would always raise sheep on the farm.

Jeff was taught the same work ethic that I had, and he was always a good worker who developed into a real handy man as he could build or repair anything. Jeff went to Tarleton for a couple of years, and then on to A&M where he graduated. He took one year of graduate studies at Texas Tech (at the same time Michelle was there), not intending to obtain a degree, but taking such courses as business law, finance, etc.

Jeff majored in agriculture economics and worked for Purina Feed for a couple of years and then was an oil lease and land man in the oil and gas business until the bust of the 1980s. Jeff had the opportunity to be a land man for the city of Abilene for the specific purpose of obtaining easements from Lake Ivie, the last large lake built in the 1980s for a supplemental or a primary water supply to Abilene. (As this book was going to press twenty years later, the pipeline was being laid from Ivie to Abilene.)

It seemed he was always busy and was not married for the first time until he was forty years old. He married Elizabeth Miller, a beautiful, tall red-head, who was a downtown manager and in economic development and is presently assistant director of community development for the city of Abilene and had previously lived in Bryan, Dallas, and Hillsboro. They married at the church near our cabin in Colorado, which was another love of Jeff's, as he spent many summers or portions of the summer in Colorado with Judge and Mimi, in addition to our stay with Michelle and Jeff during the month of July. Elizabeth's parents are deceased, and she has three brothers, Tommy, Bobby, and Billy. Her father was Bill Miller, a mechanical engineer for Carrier Bock, and her mother was Nina Wright Miller. Elizabeth's nearest relatives are her Uncle Bob Miller in Fort Worth (by the way, he is married to a Baylor graduate) and several relatives around the Livingston area, including Uncle Wayne, with whom we had the pleasure of traveling down to Livingston and speaking at their great Lions Club.

Elizabeth was also a Texas A&M graduate and quite a bit more voiced about A&M than Jeff was, who was always pretty low key. It made for some interesting conversation about Texas A&M and Baylor, and also some exciting conversation during any football game between A&M and Baylor. Nevertheless, when the teams are not playing against each other, we are pulling for the other team most of the time.

Jeff and Elizabeth converted a home on Highland in Abilene—which had been in disrepair—into a lovely home. However, soon after that, they decided to build a home six miles south of Abilene, which is in a beautiful location five miles from Buffalo Gap. They had their own designs, and Jeff was actually the contractor and used his skills to perform a lot of the work himself.

Michelle—after a great high school career in basketball, track, cheerleading, and as a winner of many other honors— went to Texas Tech. We were two Baylor graduates, and we could not get either one of them to go to Baylor (even though Jeff went to Baylor camp when he was eight or nine years old). Michelle had a successful tenure at Tech and majored in fashion merchandising and moved to Dallas, Texas, and worked for one of the department stores for a while, and then for Ann Hartley (a ladies' boutique) for several years.

She met Mark Moussa, an SMU graduate (it seemed that a lot of the Tech girls were going with the SMU graduates). They have fit right into the Dallas Highland Park area (which is the school area but, as I understand it, encompasses both University Park and Park Cities). Mark first entered a family business of imports and exports, as his father, Stanley, came from Egypt, went to school at the University of Oklahoma (sold wares out of the back of his car), and married Barbara, who was from Oklahoma. Then they settled in Dallas. Later on his father was semi-retired, and Mark and his brother George established separate businesses. Mark operates as Arteriors, Inc., from his offices in Dallas and in his showroom in Dallas, and has accessories made all over the world, mainly India and China. He has been successful in his business and has received honors in the business world and is a member of the Salesmanship Club which sponsors the Byron Nelson Golf Tournament every year and raises hundreds of thousands of dollars for children.

Dallas has been a convenient venue for us because Jay's folks lived in Fort Worth (Mr. Cowden White passed away in 1990 and Mrs. White in 2000), and Albert, Jay's brother, and Mary Jane always lived in Fort Worth since Baylor. From my interest in the Baptist church, having served as deacon and chairman on at least two occasions, and as a graduate of Baylor University, I was selected to be a member of the executive committee of the Baptist General Convention of Texas which has met three or four times a year during the past five and a half years I have been a member in addition to the meetings at the Texas Baptist General Convention.

These meetings have always been in Dallas at the Baylor Hospital. As a result, this has allowed me time for additional visits in Dallas that I might not have had under the circumstances. This has been another avenue of service. The committee actually consists of about 200 members from throughout the state and has a percentage formula for pastors and laymen. This has given me the opportunity to meet some of the finest people that are committed and dedicated to serving their fellow man, not only by missions within the state, but on the border to Mexico and throughout the world. A lot of these people give unselfishly of their time and service, as happens in the Lions Club.

The staff included Bailey Stone, a pastor in Odessa and other places, who was one of the first persons I met at Baylor University and was always an inspiration because of positive attitude and ability to preach. Phil Strickland, whom I met years ago when we were involved in a lay lawyer retreat at Salado, is still active in the Christian Life Commission and at her phases

142 LION CROSSING THE SINAI

of Baptist life. It seems the three B's have played an important role in my life: Ballinger, Baptists, and Baylor. Even though we were a year apart, Jay and I both thoroughly enjoyed Baylor and acquired many friendships, some of which have lasted for over forty years.

While at Baylor, I did continue my scouting background as I became a member of Alpha Phi Omega which was a service organization on the campus which most people called the "Glorified Boy Scouts" of college. I had great scouting experiences and completed nineteen merit badges, all but two which I lacked to become an Eagle Scout; for some reason, my attention shifted to athletics or other interests and I've always regretted that action as my dad was involved in adult scouting and I always have had an interest in scouting. In fact, I was district chairman and district commissioner of the Tri-Rivers District of the Concho Valley Scouts of the Boy Scouts of America and several of my friends at the time became Eagle Scouts as have several young friends since that time. I have always had a high regard for the scouting program. I have encouraged my grandson Tanner to become an Eagle Scout and will hopefully have the opportunity to encourage Will to become an Eagle Scout.

While at law school, I had the honor of being president of the freshmen law class, member of the board of governors, president of Phi Alpha Delta law fraternity and chosen as the outstanding graduate of Phi Alpha Delta law fraternity in 1973, some nineteen years after graduation, and also was legislative-in-cases editor of the Baylor Law Review; thereafter, I was director of the Alumni Association and Life Member Counselor of the Baylor Law School

There are six couples in the class of 1952 and 1953 that have met at homecoming every year since, I believe, 1958: Dr. Robert Henry and Pat Barfield Johnson from Brownwood (Robert Henry and Pat and Jay and I double dated on many occasions during the time we were at Baylor and we have been close friends since that time; Robert Henry is a dentist and has been my dentist and the family dentist for all these years, and Pat is still remembered for her beauty queen honors at Baylor and also being the beauty queen of the soldiers in Korea);

David and Martha Brothers from Sugarland; Delton (now deceased) and Celia Ashley from Victoria; Dr. John and LaNell Starkey from Victoria; and sometimes Pete Urban and Judy from San Antonio; Love Smith from Winters, New York, and Florida, and June Starkey, John's sister, who worked in the development office in Baylor before her recent retirement. There are various other individuals from Waco and other places who would visit our party room or brag room for our grandchildren.

Jay was instrumental, along with Gwen McLarty, in the creation and formation of the Ballinger Hospital Auxiliary, which has provided equipment and services to the hospital and medical community. Jay has been an active member of the Women's Club in Ballinger and is still involved with the programs and activities of the club. In addition, she was chairperson for the bicentennial in Ballinger in 1976, which was a three- or four-year outlay of energy and love for our country and Ballinger, Texas. The rest of the time during the 1960s and 1970s, she was a housewife and a mother, but for some thirty-seven years has primarily been a supporter, a traveler, engaging in Lions activities.

She did teach in Brady the year of our marriage as she graduated before I got out of law school. We thought it would be a good idea for her to become accustomed to West Texas, and she was able to get a job in Brady with Superintendent Reynolds. Jay absolutely fell in love with Brady because it is a small town like Ballinger, and the people there were friendly. She rented a room or apartment from Lucille Benham who was familiar with all of the people in Brady. We were married on April 3rd of that year, while she was still teaching and living in Brady, and we took our honeymoon in Monterrey, Mexico, on a long weekend.

We were expecting the army duty call any day, even though the wedding had been planned for some time. She would come to Ballinger on the weekends, unless she had a school activity, and I would go to Brady on Wednesday nights. It worked out well, especially since it was only a couple of months before I would head for the army. I could not have had a better soundbox than Jay as she has the knack of knowing people by her ideas, likes, and dislikes, and she is one of the most caring and compassionate people I have ever known.

And My Legal Family . . .

In addition to my original partner, Judge Grindstaff, I have been most fortunate to have two other partners, Don Reese and Ken Slimp—thus "Grindstaff, Grindstaff and Reese" and then "Grindstaff, Grindstaff and Slimp."

In 1976 we thought there was a need for an office in Winters because of aging lawyers there. Don Reese, a product of San Angelo Central High School, Abilene Christian University, and Texas Tech Law School (who had practiced in Lubbock for two years), wanted to come home to West Texas. He fit in perfectly in Winters and is an intelligent, firm, and caring lawyer.

Don left after a couple of years to work for an oil company in Abilene, but I have worked with him in oil and gas leases and title work. Don and Lisa Curnutt now have an LLP title company in Abilene. But ever since 1979 we have treated each other as partners, with exchange of information and fees. Don is a lawyer's lawyer—honest, the epitome of integrity, and a true family man along with wife Linda.

In 1979, knowing that my legal time was going to be restricted by as much as seventy-five to ninety percent one year, I needed another lawyer to assist Judge and the six secretaries we were using. A TCU "Froggie" (but at least he went to Baylor Law School) came our way and fit the bill for our office in Winters—small town climate, great place to raise a family with Mary Slimp, graduate of Baylor Business School.

Ken was a loyal associate and great researcher who also became city attorney of Winters where he has served in that capacity to the present and also assistant district attorney for San Angelo district which includes Winters and Ballinger, for some ten years as of this writing. (Steve Smith, district attorney in San Angelo, is also a Baylor graduate—whose dad was a true Lion in Mississippi.)

Legal secretaries who assisted me during high times of absence were Saam Geistman, who later moved to the Winters office; Rhonda Goetz, a secretary for twelve years during my Lionistic career, who became an executive assistant and parale-

gal without the formal title (with one of the most positive attitudes in life and who exuded enthusiasm and rapport with all
clients); Monnie Davis, legal secretary with us for fourteen years
as of this writing, who had no training in business or legal procedures but took hold and exhibited confidence and intelligence
and is a great diplomat over the phone and to all our clients in
person; Rose Marie Englert, who was a high school trainee in
our Winters office in the early 1980s and later joined the office
in March 2000 and has quickly climbed the ladder to become a
legal secretary who can act in my absence.

Twenty years ago I began to hire students after school from
the Distributive Education program for typing and filing and
running errands. I started calling them my "legal eagles," and
some of them during the busy years of Lions travels included
Kathy Slaughter, Karol Spreen, Lacy Binder, Carrie Howe, and
Lori Schaeffer, all who were unique in their own way but provided the service and efficiency that was desired.

Four of them went on to A&M University, including Jamie
McWright (now in public relations in Houston after a stint in
Washington), and her sister Julie McWright (who underwent
health problems but toughed it out), Holly, the daughter of Rose
and Robert Englert, who earned an outstanding student scholarship for four years at A&M where she began her first day as we
were finalizing this book manuscript, and Cali Dill (pronounced
"kay-lee," which took me a year to learn to pronounce) moving
into her second year with my office and who also is the captain
of the flag corps and won fourth in state in feature writing as a
junior.

Mixed in was the only male "legal eagle," Wade Edington,
who performed the same tasks as the girls and even went to feed
the sheep when I was out of town; he worked for a lawyer his first
year at Angelo State and was at Texas Tech as of this writing.

And the new "kid" in the office as of this writing was Kelly
Travis, a very personable cheerleader and participant in other
extracurricular events.

The employment of these students was the best move that
I ever made in the legal field because they not only provided efficient service and had the opportunity to meet other people in
a business atmosphere, but I had the good fortune of hiring top

young people in Ballinger High School, both in scholarship, activities and personalities.

"Tankeye" Then and Now

I'll never forget one of my early appearances as International President in far-away Kuala Lumpur, where I presented the Lions International "Head of State Award" to Prime Minister Datuk Seri Dr. Mahathir Muhamad for oustanding humanitarian service in the prevention of drug abuse. He was the third leader in the world to receive the award that year—the others being President Ronald Reagan and President Zia Ul Haq of Pakistan. (The "Head of State Award" had previously been presented to Anwar Sadat and Menachem Begin).

Another memorable event was when Jay and I arrived in Karachi, Pakistan, on an overnight flight from Rome. It had been one of those flights that was not very pleasant because of the storms and other elements that knocked us around. I did not enjoy that flight, and Jay certainly did not. However, we arrived in Karachi at 5 A.M. We were combing hair and fixing faces quickly as we walked toward the front door, and both had mentioned that it was time to put on our best face even though there might not be many people there.

As the doors of the plane opened, there were some three hundred people present, including Assai Dossani, the district governor, and it looked like at least half or more of the people were in attire that indicated they, too, had walked across the desert in order to be present on that occasion. It was not Ebb and Jay Grindstaff; it was the president and first lady of Lions Clubs International, and they would have given any president the same welcome.

We threw the bags in the car and dropped off the bags at the hotel but did not leave the car. This was the day of observance for activities and the education of activities of the Pakistanian Lions. (Little did we know that in 1999 the first female director of Lions Club International would be from Pakistan: Nilofer Bakhtiar).

At twelve minutes after six, our host told us that Lions Club International had informed them that the guests should have a little time for rest, and they would pick us up for the formal affair at six thirty. I don't know how we did it, it seemed like the activities of the day gave us the adrenaline to keep on going.

During the course of the afternoon, we were taken to a bank. In this room was a blood bank, an eye bank, and a crutch bank. Seated at the head table was the president of the project and/or club and the district governor; there were probably thirty people or so in the room. They were explaining their project and how it worked with great enthusiasm.

I observed a gentleman standing or leaning in the corner who appeared to be decrepit, had long, unkempt hair, one tooth that I could see and it may had been the only tooth; I wondered what part he played in the program or the project.

About that time, they asked me if I would participate in the crutch bank program, and I said, "Sure, what can I do?" They said, "We want you to present a crutch to someone." I said O.K. We got up, I had the crutch, and they brought the man who only had one leg to the center of the room. I put the crutch under his arm and he looked up at me and said, "Tankye." He had probably practiced this particular part of the program for months. I will never forget his face or his eyes of gratitude. And then he walked across the room to the door with the one crutch under his arm and stepped down on the first step and then turned around and again said, "Tankye."

How could you express it any better?

"Tankye" for taking the time to read this book of experiences and leadership and values and life, and I hope that it has provoked some thought and certainly some attitude of humor that we must have in our journey. More importantly, I would like to take this opportunity to say Tankye for all the grass-root Lions who gave time and assets in an unselfish manner in order that they might improve the lives of someone less fortunate.

Index